ROBIN SCROGGS

The New Testament and Homosexuality

CONTEXTUAL BACKGROUND FOR CONTEMPORARY DEBATE

FORTRESS PRESS   PHILADELPHIA

ALSO BY ROBIN SCROGGS

Paul for a New Day

Library of Congress Cataloging in Publication Data

Scroggs, Robin.
  The New Testament and homosexuality.

  Includes index.
    1. Homosexuality—Biblical teaching. 2. Homo-
sexuality—History. 3. Sociology, Biblical.
4. Bible. N.T.—Criticism, interpretation, etc.
I. Title.
BS2545.H63S37   1983   261.8'35766   82–48588
ISBN 0–8006–0699–X

9770A83   Printed in the United States of America   1–699

Contents

Preface

As all authors know, but perhaps few readers, books are often generated out of situations which may seem at the time to be purely accidental—a chance personal meeting, the influence of a book that one had not intended to read, and so forth. Four years ago I would never have imagined myself addressing this topic in book form. But, about that time, I attended a meeting of church leaders, ministers, and lay persons, solely as a guest. One of the items on the agenda was a report by an ad hoc committee which presented a resolution concerning the issue of civil rights for homosexual persons. The discussion this report caused was sharp and even bitter in tone. I sat amazed as I heard the Bible being invoked in ways that were wholly inappropriate to any canons of biblical scholarship. Perhaps something in me snapped during those minutes. For better or worse, I decided that somebody needed somehow to provide resources that would give both clarity and honesty: clarity about the real issues with which the Bible dealt, and honesty about how the Bible could or could not appropriately inform the current debate. For better or worse, I decided I would lay aside some other long-range research plans in order to come to terms with the issues explored in the following pages.

Perhaps this "personal confession" will signal my own interests and involvement with the topic. I am not a homosexual. Nor do I write this book as an advocate either for or against the ecclesiastical rights of homosexuals. I confess to a confusion about the merits of psychological arguments concerning homosexual inclinations, a confusion I know I share with many people. I just do not know whether homosexuality is or can be normal or whether it can be as fulfilling to the human person as heterosexuality.

At the same time I confess equally that I see no way of reading the Christian gospel except that it is one which totally accepts in love all persons, regardless of inadequacies or moral failings. And I have seen too many tragic rejections of homosexual persons in the name of Christian righteousness or even love. I thus offer these pages in the hope that, in addition to bringing clarity and honesty to issues of the relevance of the Bible, it may bring as well a little more light and a little less heat to the discussion, a little more acceptance of all persons on the "other side," and maybe even an awareness that in Christ there is really no "other side" at all.

Ultimately, however, my purpose in writing is to make it as clear as possible what are the issues in the use of the Bible in Christian debates about the acceptance of homosexuals. Just what is a proper use of the Bible, especially the New Testament, in these discussions? If this is the basic question of the book, the reader may experience some surprise and, perhaps, frustration in learning that most of the pages which follow are concerned with nonbiblical materials. Why do I deal so extensively with Greek, Roman, and early Jewish texts? Why do I not simply explore what the biblical texts themselves say?

There have, in fact, been a number of recent studies of the biblical texts. Most of them, however, remain so close to exegesis of the texts themselves that they do not explore the wider societal context. That is, they do not raise the question: *What are the authors against?*[1] What are they opposing when they oppose homosexuality? Yet this is, in fact, the very first question that should be asked and answered! If one wants to know the *meaning* of a prohibition, one must first determine just what it is the author of the prohibition is against. It seems to be assumed by most that homosexuality in the time of the New Testament must have been the same as it is now—surely this seems obvious. But it is the most serious violation of any scholarly canon to assume without inspection that what an ancient author is opposed to is the same phenomenon as exists in our own time.

---

1. Two recent happy exceptions are the works of V. P. Furnish, *The Moral Teaching of Paul: Selected Issues* (Nashville: Abingdon Press, 1979), pp. 52–83, and John Boswell, *Christianity, Social Tolerance, and Homosexuality* (Chicago: Univ. of Chicago Press, 1980), pp. 61–87, 335–53.

What *is* the model of homosexuality to which biblical authors were opposed? For persons involved in the current debate, charged, perhaps, with making decisions about the acceptance of homosexuals in the church, it would be crucial for them to know the answer to this question. But how can these persons know if scholarship withholds the answer? I have consulted numerous commentaries on the relevant passages in the New Testament (there are only three of them) to see what the minister or lay person might learn. I was shocked to find that virtually none of them offered any adequate information. Either the authors did not know or they considered it too indelicate to go into the detail necessary to communicate the reality of the context to the reader. I assume the reason is the latter. But if so, they have done a great disservice to us, since they have let us remain in ignorance about what the New Testament is against, and thus have made it impossible for us to know how the Bible may or may not be properly used in today's discussions.

After an initial review of the contemporary discussion, I raise the question about the cultural realities of the world of the New Testament. This necessitates a detailed exploration of the Greco-Roman culture of homosexuality, which we will see was defined by the model of *pederasty*, the love and use of boys or youths by adult males.[2] I next describe early Jewish responses to pagan homosexual culture, so that we might better understand the attitudes of Jewish Christians (for instance, Paul). Only when this absolutely necessary spadework is done is it even possible to discuss the New Testament texts, and *then only and always in relation to the cultural context* out of which the texts emerged.

In the final chapter, I give my own judgments about the proper use of the Bible. I need, perhaps, to forewarn the reader that my ultimate conclusions may seem negative. This is not, however, due to any disrespect I have for the biblical message. Indeed, as a

2. It must be admitted that although I constantly use the phrase "Greco-Roman culture" when speaking of the background of the New Testament, I lean much more heavily on Greek texts than Roman. This is in large part because of the commonality of language with the New Testament. Fortunately, Boswell's work balances the description in my book with many references to Latin literature, cf. especially *Christianity, Social Tolerance, and Homosexuality*, pp. 61–87. Both cultures, however, had similar practices and attitudes.

scholar of the New Testament I have devoted my entire professional life to seek a better understanding of that message, first of all for my own growth and life, and then to communicate that understanding to others. No, my seemingly negative conclusions are not because of disrespect but for the opposite reason: continued invocation of the biblical injunctions in the current debate violates, in my judgment, the integrity of the biblical authors themselves. Thus if I take an advocacy role in this book, it is for a proper use of Scripture which does not violate its integrity.

Since my aim is to communicate to nonspecialists, I have attempted to write in a nontechnical fashion and have done what I could to eliminate detailed, complicated matters from discussion. I have also tried to avoid strewing the pages with technical terms or with unnecessary Greek or Hebrew words. Some use of such terms and words is, of course, unavoidable. I have, furthermore, cited, where possible, Greek and Roman authors from the Loeb Classical Library (LCL), published by Harvard University Press and William Heinemann, since these texts and translations are readily available in libraries for inspection. Finally, I need to add that I am myself but an amateur about Greek and Roman literature. To the best of my awareness, what I say in this area is accurate and supportable. If a reader more knowledgeable than I finds assertions which are not finely tuned to the sensitivities of the expert, I ask his or her indulgence.

Professors William Klassen and Robert Bennett have read the manuscript in whole or part and given me valuable criticisms. Kathryn van Voorst helped me with the final editing process. Marlene Woodson typed the final copy with care and diligence. For all these people I extend my sincere appreciation. As for everything important to my life, I am indebted to my wife, Marilee, for her sustained and understanding support throughout this time.

ROBIN SCROGGS
Ash Wednesday, 1982

1
The Use of the Bible
in Recent Church Discussions
about Homosexuality

The main purpose of this book will be to describe the practices of and attitudes toward homosexuality in the Greco-Roman world. This is the case because Christian statements about homosexuality in the New Testament are responses to that cultural scene. Until we know what the biblical authors were against we cannot begin to reflect upon the relevance of those writings for contemporary issues. This is the consistent logic of my argument, and it will necessitate a careful reading of the following chapters, however little one may think he or she is interested in Greco-Roman culture on this issue. Once this is done, of course, we will then turn our attention to the biblical pronouncements, concentrating primarily on passages in the New Testament as reactions to the cultural reality surrounding the early church. First, however, it is helpful to get some orientation to the contemporary debates. We need to keep in mind (a) what is being concluded and (b) how the Bible informs and influences the decisions that are being made. What follows is illustrative and makes no attempt to be exhaustive or current. It will at least provide us with an entree into the uses and abuses of the Bible in the current discussions within the churches about homosexuality. I think, even in this brief survey, that it will be readily apparent that most of the arguments just simply assume the identity of homosexuality then and homosexuality now. To be sure, such debate has not (yet) occurred in all denominations. In some cases this may be due to a tacit acceptance of homosexual persons. In others it may be due to such an overwhelming revulsion against such acceptance that the issue is suppressed and remains in the closet.

1

Where the issue has surfaced, however, discussion has often been polarized and the tone angry. The courage of homosexual persons to "come out of the closet" and the support often given them by their heterosexual friends has provided a clear target for others who proclaim that homosexuality is contrary to the will of God. Sometimes these latter are charged in rebuttal with "homophobia," a rather poor coinage, but now accepted as a term denoting irrational fear of homosexuality. This discussion may be exemplified by recent events within three "mainline" Protestant denominations.

DENOMINATIONAL DEBATE

1. *The United Church of Christ.* In 1977 a study volume, *Human Sexuality: A Preliminary Study*, was prepared by a committee for discussion at the Eleventh General Synod (1977) of the UCC.[1] The report is wide-ranging, dealing with biblical, psychological, political, and ecclesiastical perspectives. It is not primarily concerned with homosexuality, although the issue is explicitly raised at appropriate places. I think it fair to characterize the tone of the report as "liberal"; that is, it makes no explicit condemnation of specific sexual activities, except from the broadly based perspective that love should guide all kinds of relationships. The biblical passages are placed in the historical context of the times in which they were written; they are not taken as divinely uttered, eternally valid ethical pronouncements. In a sentence that highlights this perspective the report states: "It would be a mistake merely to transplant isolated statements out of the context of the New Testament in the modern world and thus twist their meanings to fit situations quite different from those to which they were originally addressed."[2]

Although the General Synod received the report (without discussion of the contents) for the purpose of further study and response within the denomination, some delegates quickly reacted against the "limited theological, biblical, and ethical viewpoint re-

1. *Human Sexuality: A Preliminary Study* (United Church Board for Homeland Ministries, 1977).
2. Ibid., p. 64.

flected in the Study."[3] A caucus which grew out of this reaction published what amounts to a rebuttal, in a collection of essays entitled *Issues in Sexual Ethics*.[4] Here strong exception is taken at least to the implications of *Human Sexuality: A Preliminary Study*, and particular attention is paid to the issue of homosexuality (far more so than in the original document itself). Homosexuality is here identified as a sin in very forthright fashion. God has spoken in his Word, and the issue is settled by that Word, regardless of other kinds of consideration. "The Christian homosexual position when carefully examined can be exposed for what it is at its very core: an attack upon the integrity, sufficiency, and authority of Scripture, which for the Christian Church is an attack upon the very nature of our Holy God."[5]

Thus the issue has been joined in the denomination. Currently the UCC is embarked in a several-year process of study and debate, and no denominational decision is expected in the near future. The sentences I have quoted indicate that the Bible plays an important role on both sides of the debate. They equally demonstrate how differently the biblical text is being used.

2. *The United Methodist Church*. This denomination has, in distinction from the UCC, a clearly stated policy about homosexuality. In the 1980 *Discipline* the following statement is made: "Further we insist that all persons are entitled to have their human and civil rights ensured, though we do not condone the practice of homosexuality and consider this practice incompatible with Christian teaching."[6] The UMC has explicitly prohibited any use of its funds for the support of gay caucuses or homosexuality in general.[7] And while *The Discipline* does not explicitly deny ordination to homosexual persons, the language used to define the character and moral standards necessary for ordination can be taken so to exclude such persons.[8]

3. A statement from "The Minority Resolution Recognized by the Eleventh General Synod," published in M. Duffy, ed., *Issues in Sexual Ethics* (Souderton, Pa.: United Church People for Biblical Witness, 1979), p. 189.
4. Ibid.
5. Nuermberger, "Good News for the Homosexual," Ibid., p. 127.
6. *The Book of Discipline of the United Methodist Church* (Nashville: The United Methodist Pub. House, 1980), paragraph 71, p. 90.
7. Ibid., paragraph 906, no. 13, p. 386.
8. Ibid., paragraph 404, pp. 181f. Cf. especially note 2, beginning on p. 182.

In recent action the 1980 General Conference voted to circulate a very brief study document on human sexuality.[9] It calls for reappraisals of traditional views about sexual life styles and for the avoidance of moralistic judgment on those whose styles are different. It deplores homophobia[10] and urges "the Church to resist easy moralisms or dogmatic views which set up different views regarding the 'normalcy' in sexual behavior of heterosexuality and homosexuality."[11] In this particular document the Bible is virtually unmentioned. The appeal is to love and the sense of human dignity rather than to biblical norms. Only the following sentence draws upon the biblical traditions. "The Bible reflects the ambiguities we experience in our human sexuality. Yet its message about creation, sin, judgment and redemption is that God is good, loving, and just and will sustain us in our brokenness as well as in our strength."[12] This statement is itself ambiguous and perhaps reveals a general uneasiness within the denomination about the appropriate use of the Bible.

3. *The United Presbyterian Church.* Probably it is safe to say that the denomination that has given most careful attention to the place of homosexuals within the church is the United Presbyterian Church. In 1977 an appointed Task Force assembled many individual documents for its study as well as for general distribution within the denomination.[13] This committee was charged with bringing to the 1978 General Assembly recommendations concerning the ordination of homosexual persons. The procedure was established in response to a request by one Presbytery for "definitive guidance" on the matter from General Assembly.

The Task Force prepared a two-hundred-page document, which is in part a detailed study guide on biblical and ecclesiastical

---

9. "Study Document on Human Sexuality," in *The Book of Resolutions of the United Methodist Church* (Nashville: The United Methodist Pub. House, 1980), pp. 146–152.

10. Ibid., p. 151.

11. Ibid. The sentence is somewhat opaque. The context indicates it means that homosexuality should not necessarily be seen as more promiscuous or otherwise more evil than heterosexuality.

12. Ibid.

13. I refer to "Packet 2" of the material, dated July 1, 1977, under the letterhead of the United Presbyterian Church, General Assembly Mission Council.

issues.[14] All of the biblical passages which might be relevant are studied carefully. It is clear that the issue of biblical authority was a weighty one in the deliberations of the Task Force. In fact the study identifies four separate views of the authority of Scripture said to be found among Presbyterians and describes what the implications might be for judgments on homosexuality based on these differing views.

The Task Force reported both a majority and a minority recommendation to the 1978 General Assembly. The burden of the majority recommendation was to sidestep the requested denominational decree by leaving the decision about ordination of homosexual persons to each Presbytery, in which, it was noted, the rights to ordain have traditionally lain. The brunt of the minority report was to recommend that the denomination declare that "self-affirming, practicing" homosexual persons should be denied ordination not only to the professional ministry (in Presbyterian terminology, "teaching elder") but also to those ministries of "ruling elder" (in other denominations they would be lay elders, board members, etc.) and "deacon." The minority report leans heavily on Scripture for its judgment and authority. "We anchor our understanding of homosexuality in the revelation of God's intention for our own life in Scripture and Christ's living Spirit."[15] "For the church to ordain an avowed practicing homosexual to the ministry of the Word and Sacrament would be to act in contradiction to her charter and calling in Scripture. . . ."[16]

Once the General Assembly convened in 1978, the document prepared by the Task Force was given, as is customary in such cases, to an entirely different committee of the Assembly. This group was charged with bringing recommendations to the floor and was not bound in any way by the conclusions of the Task Force. While elements of both majority and minority recommendations were incorporated in the final version presented to the floor and passed by the Assembly, substantively the minority view

14. Contained in *Blue Book 1*, 190th General Assembly (1978) of the United Presbyterian Church: D-1–201.
15. Ibid., p. D-188.
16. Ibid., p. D-193.

became victorious. As a result the Assembly voted to give "definitive guidance" to its Presbyteries: "That unrepentant homosexual practice does not accord with the requirements for ordination set forth in Form of Government, Chapter VII, Section 3 (37.03):
[namely] 'It is indispensable that, besides possessing the necessary gifts and abilities, natural and acquired, everyone undertaking a particular ministry should have a sense of inner persuasion, be sound in the faith, live according to godliness, have the approval of God's people and the concurring judgment of a lawful judicatory of the Church.'"[7] It should be noted that "ordination" above includes teaching elders, ruling elders, and deacons. Hence not only may an "unrepentant homosexual" not become a professional clergyperson, he or she may not serve on the major boards of individual churches.[18]

These are merely a few examples of a church discussion which has probably only just begun. The issue has emerged, and will emerge in other denominations, in individual churches throughout the land, and in theological seminaries. It is not even certain that debate is over for the Methodists and Presbyterians. In part this debate in the church is only reflective of similar perplexities in the larger society. Church members can be as uncertain of the "normalcy" of homosexuals as can the secular person, equally unclear as to the status of various psychological and sociological theories. And church members can be as guilty of "homophobia" as anybody else.

In the church, however, there is a crucial question which is not asked in nonreligious circles: Is homosexuality contrary to the will of God? What counts, however, as evidence for the will of God? At this point the Bible assumes center stage, for the Bible has traditionally been that central locus where the church has found revealed the will of God. Certainly, for most people it is not the only locus of revelation. There is church reflection over the centu-

17. *The Church and Homosexuality* (New York: Office of the General Assembly, 1978), p. 61.
18. The words "unrepentant" and "practicing" are crucial here in understanding the action of the General Assembly. A homosexual who concludes that his sexual orientation is wrong and turns to a heterosexual perspective, as well as a homosexual who, despite his feelings, can commit him or herself to celibacy are eligible for ordination. Cf. ibid., p. 60.

ries; there are insights from secular disciplines; there is human experience or the guidance of the Spirit. Yet the Bible retains pride of place and its judgments cannot be avoided by anyone, if only because there are so many believers for whom it is the sole and sufficient revelation. Thus even the so-called liberal, for whom the findings of human experience in such disciplines as psychology and sociology are crucial, and for whom the Bible may appear in part to be so culture-and time-bound as to be discardable on many specific issues, must come to terms with the biblical message and, as persuasively as possible, explain why he or she does *not* interpret or value its message as do others.

Thus it is important to gain as much clarity about how the Bible has been used, how it should or should not be used, not as an academic exercise but as preparation for the long debate that has already begun and must surely continue. Each of us needs to know *why* we hold the views we do and what are the implications and presuppositions of our views. At the same time we need to hear sympathetically the views of others who differ, to understand the logic of their positions. What we need is a little less heat and a little more light. It is to this goal that our thought should be directed. Consequently, in the following section I will explore some of the ways in which the Bible has been used in the debate that has taken place up to this time.

THE APPROPRIATION OF THE BIBLE
The Bible Opposes Homosexuality[19]

The great majority of interpreters do believe or assume that at several places the Bible quite clearly opposes homosexuality. Not all such interpreters, however, use this judgment in the same way when applying it to the contemporary debate. Thus our first task is to assess how those who *do* think the Bible opposes homosexuality relate this presumed fact to contemporary discussions.

1. *The Bible opposes homosexuality and is definitive for what the church should think and do about it.* Here the Bible stands as the objective revelation of God's eternal will. The judgments in Leviticus and in

19. For detailed discussions of the passages mentioned in this section, cf. chapters 5 and 7.

the New Testament make it completely clear that God is opposed to homosexuality. Within this broad category there are a number of variations, often quite subtle, which cannot be explored here. In all variations, however, the conclusion is the same: Homosexual activity is sinful and church members who practice homosexuality must be called to repentance. Ordination to the professional ministry is not permissible. As one statement expresses it, "Therefore, in accordance with God's word as found in Paul and Leviticus, the church should plainly label all homosexual behavior as sin. . . . "[20] Or even more sharply put: "At its core, homosexuality is rebellion against God's authority and established order, and idolatry of the worst variety."[21]

2. *The Bible opposes homosexuality, but it is just one sin among many. There is no justification for singling it out as more serious than other sins castigated in the Bible, but because of which ordination is not denied.* Among those who maintain this position, the point is frequently made that there are extremely few references to homosexuality in the pages of the Bible. Furthermore, the statements in Leviticus, 1 Corinthians and 1 Timothy attach this sin to numerous others. This is even true of Romans 1, where after the attack on homosexuality Paul makes his most extensive list of vices, which, interestingly enough, itself makes no mention of homosexuality.

Proponents of this view do not want to avoid saying that homosexuality is a sin. They do seem, however, to wish to relativize the apparently unique significance given to this one sin by proponents of view 1. The stricture in Leviticus, for example, is contained in a list of sins of forms of incest, child sacrifice, intercourse with a menstruating woman, and bestiality. The list in 1 Corinthians includes adulterers, thieves, the greedy, and drunkards. 1 Timothy lists, among others, liars and perjurers. By what logic is homosexuality lifted out from among these other sins? "In none of the passages is homosexuality as such singled out as a special kind of sin."[22] Not everyone, it is pointed out, would consider intercourse with a menstruating woman a sin of any sort. Denominations have not (yet) sought to determine which candidates for

20. This is given as one possible position in *Church and Homosexuality*, p. 29.
21. Nuermberger, *Issues in Sexual Ethics*, p. 132.
22. *Human Sexuality*, p. 63.

ordination are greedy and to exclude from ordination all such thought to be. Homosexuals should, perhaps, be called to repentance, but only within the broad context of the church's condemnation of all sin. Adherents to this view do not necessarily espouse ordination for homosexual persons; but the logic of their argument does leave them that option.[23]

3. *The Bible opposes homosexuality but the specific injunctions must be placed in the larger biblical context of the theology of creation, sin, judgment, and grace.* Here the argument in its logical form is that the prohibitions about homosexuality should not be isolated from the basic theological affirmations which are central to the Judeo-Christian tradition. This functions similarly to a hermeneutical principle used by Luther, among others, and can be called the "analogy of faith." According to this principle, the heart of the Bible is its central message(s)—however the interpreter decides what is central. This primary gospel is then used as a principle to evaluate other more specific or less essential parts of Scripture. If these parts are consonant with the central message, they can be accepted; if not, they may be ignored or judged inferior to the primary revelation.[24] Specific application of this argument can take several different directions and has been used both by opponents and proponents of the acceptance of homosexuals within the church and its ecclesiastical structures.

(*a*) The argument from biblical narrations of creation. In this case the Genesis narration of the creation into male and female, with the joining of the two in sexual union, is said to portray God's intention for the relationship of male and female. This is the positive statement about heterosexuality in Scripture which complements and puts into perspective the injunctions against any sort of deviation from that intent (as in Leviticus and Ro-

23. Again the word "unrepentant" is important at this point. It could be argued that a candidate who openly advocated greediness, or any of the other sins spoken against in Scripture, should quite properly be denied ordination. A person who sees nothing wrong in greediness is then on the same level as a person who sees nothing wrong in homosexual practices.

24. For an interesting application of this principle to the issue of the Bible's views toward women, cf. Paul Jewett, *Man as Male and Female* (Grand Rapids: Wm. B. Erdmans, 1975). From the perspective of this author Jesus' accepting attitude toward women takes priority over views of female subordination expressed in part of the Pauline corpus.

mans). As the document adopted by the UPC General Assembly in 1978 states: "As we examine the whole framework of teaching bearing upon our sexuality from Genesis onward, we find that homosexuality is a contradiction of God's wise and beautiful pattern for human sexual relationships. . . . It is a confusion of sexual roles that mirrors the tragic inversion in which men and women worship the creature instead of the Creator."[25]

(*b*) The argument from the principle of love. There is, of course, no theologian who fails to appeal to the norm of love in the Christian tradition, love from God and love to and from the neighbor. There is probably no denominational statement on homosexuality, of whatever view, which does not appeal in one way or another to the importance of love and loving. Nevertheless, this appeal is particularly useful to those who take a moderating or so-called liberal view toward homosexuals in the church. A clear example can be found in the UCC study report, although the reader must keep in mind that the report is addressing all issues of sexuality. The initiating sentence in the section on the New Testament reads: "'God is love' is the central affirmation of biblical faith which forms the context in which all Scripture must be interpreted."[26] This norm is then applied to biblical judgments on homosexuality. "It would be a mistake merely to transplant isolated statements out of the context of the New Testament in the modern world and thus twist their meanings to fit situations quite different from those to which they were originally addressed. Christians can and should take *basic biblical convictions* and use them as resources for discovering and cultivating those human relationships which affirm life and love, support persons and edify wholesome human relationships."[27] Thus the believer is free and called to responsibility to make an *independent* judgment about what counts as "human relationships which affirm life and love." In the name of the Bible, the Bible can be critiqued.[28]

25. *Church and Homosexuality*, p. 58. The reference to idolatry shows the authors also have Romans 1 in mind.
26. *Human Sexuality*, p. 57.
27. Ibid., p. 64. Italics mine.
28. Among contemporary, as well as classical theologians and scholars, this procedure is quite common. People of this persuasion believe that the Bible is not completely consistent nor are all its parts of equal value. Most will admit that they operate with a "canon within the canon," i.e., take certain parts as more authoritative than others.

4. *The Bible opposes homosexuality but is so time- and culture-bound that its injunctions may and should be discarded if other considerations suggest better alternatives.* Other considerations might, of course, include arguments from the analogy of faith (position 3) but they may also come from contemporary theological, psychological, or sociological reflections. If Leviticus and Paul are addressing situations so foreign to our own times, there is no reason to apply those judgments as determinative in our own situation. The observation might be made that homosexual relationships can be shown to be as helpful and caring to the participants as heterosexual. If that should seem to be the case, the biblical injunctions should not influence our decisions.

When outlining possible options that could be taken by Presbyterians, the UPC Task Force described one option as follows. "Sexual orientation does not itself determine a person's capacity for love, beauty, and joy. Sexual orientation does not itself define one's relationship to God. A homosexuality that issues in faithful, tender, respectful, hopeful, and mutually fulfilling acts is an instrument of love, beauty, and joy. As such it is moral."[29]

Even this brief sketch of positions shows that people can agree about the meaning of biblical statements and yet differ widely as to how they should be applied to the contemporary debate. Obviously what is at issue, then, is not interpretation of the Bible per se (i.e., exegesis), but extrabiblical theological judgments about the authority of Scripture (i.e., hermeneutics). It may be that differences at this level are the ultimate source of tensions about the proper use of Scripture in the debate. That it may be possible for people with such different theological perspectives to agree on the proper role of the Bible in the debate is a hope, at least, to which I shall return at the end of the book.

The Bible Does Not Oppose Homosexuality

In recent years a few adventurous interpreters have boldly claimed that the Bible actually does not oppose homosexuality. Here we are clearly in a different kind of argument, now not over the hermeneutical principles of the application of Scripture but over the directly interpretive task of determining just what Scrip-

29. *Blue Book*, 1, p. D–99.

ture says. In the first instance below, however, the primary tool is psychological.

1. *The Bible does not oppose homosexuality because it does not speak of true or innate homosexuality but rather of homosexual acts by people who are not homosexuals.* A person may be born, so the argument runs, with a homosexual orientation—or at least is directed toward same-sex fulfillment from his or her earliest days. By those who begin with this judgment such a person may be called an *invert*. He or she may or may not engage in homosexual acts. In contrast, a *pervert* is said to be a person who engages in acts contrary to his or her orientation.[30] Thus a heterosexual person who engages in homosexual activity is a pervert, just as a homosexual person would be who engages in heterosexual acts. While there does not appear to be agreement amongst psychologists or sociologists as to cause, there is broad agreement among some of them that "the genuine homosexual condition, or *inversion*, . . . is something for which the subject can in no way be held responsible. . . . "[31]

The distinction between inversion and perversion is then applied to the relevant biblical texts. "Strictly speaking, the Bible and Christian tradition know nothing of *homosexuality*; both are concerned solely with the commission of homosexual *acts*. . . ."[32] Or a similar statement by Seward Hiltner: "At least in its reference to homosexuality, therefore, the Bible does not speak at all to the principal way in which homosexuality must be understood today."[33] If this is so, then the Bible is clearly irrelevant for the contemporary discussion and cannot be used to argue for or against the acceptance or ordination of homosexuals.

2. *The Bible does not oppose homosexuality because the texts do not deal with homosexuality in general.* Here the key phrase is "in general." Homosexuality may be frowned upon, but the real reason for the

30. Cf. D. S. Bailey, *Homosexuality and the Western Christian Tradition* (New York and London: Longmans, Green & Co., 1955), pp. x–xi; John McNeill, *The Church and the Homosexual* (Kansas City, Kansas: Sheed Andrews and McMeel, 1976), p. 42. In earlier psychology these terms are not so neatly separated from one another. I am not entirely sure where lies the origin of the distinction made by Bailey.
31. Bailey, *Homosexuality and the Western Christian Tradition*, p. **xi**.
32. Ibid., p. x.
33. Seward Hiltner, *Bulletin of the Christian Association for Psychological Studies* 3/4 (1977): 4. Cited in *Issues in Sexual Ethics*, p. 126.

biblical injunction lies elsewhere. Again the reader must wait until later chapters to see the detailed exegetical investigations. Here only the conclusions can be listed. Deut. 23:17–18 inveighs against female and male cult prostitutes. But it is at least a strong option that the male prostitute serviced females rather than males. Thus "the KJV [King James Version] translation 'sodomite' has no contemporary scholarly basis and must be judged a mistranslation."[34] Even if such a male did service other males, it is prostitution per se which is prohibited, not homosexuality in general.

Lev. 18:22 and 20:13 clearly legislate against male homosexuality. But why? Is the objection purely sexual, or is it otherwise? One possible answer is that the basic objection is to the wasting of male semen. As the UCC study guide says: "The condemnation of male homosexual acts must be seen in the context of the procreative ethic which it served."[35] Thus the law may be primarily directed not against same-sex relationships in and of themselves but rather against the *result* of male homosexuality. Since today "wasting of semen" may not be considered a sin at all, the contemporary relevance of the law is nullified.

Similarly these laws can be seen as directed primarily against foreign religious practices. If so, then the separation of Israel from "the nations" and not primarily some horror of homosexuality in itself is the purpose of the prohibitions. Tom Horner defends his view and concludes: "What we do know about these Levitical writers in respect to their aversion to homosexuality is that this aversion was cultic in origin. . . . "[36] The UCC study guide raises this same possibility, although it prefers not to answer its own question. "The question is whether the code forbade homosexual acts because they were wrong per se, because they violated the procreative ethic, or because they were involved with idolatry?"[37]

Even more popular has been the attempt to deny that the sin of Sodom described in Genesis 19 was sexual in nature. The evil as-

34. *Blue Book*, 1, p. D–39.
35. *Human Sexuality*, p. 54.
36. Tom Horner, *Jonathan Loved David: Homosexuality in Biblical Times* (Philadelphia: Westminster Press, 1978), p. 85.
37. *Human Sexuality*, p. 56.

cribed to the cities in later Jewish and Christian traditions is not homosexuality. Rather, when the sin is identified, it is lack of hospitality. The citizens do not want to "know" the angels in a sexual sense; their aim is to identify just who these strangers are and perhaps to eject them from their city. As D. S. Bailey summarizes this view: "The association of homosexual practices with the Sodom story is a late and *extrinsic* feature which, for some reason, has been read into the original account."[38] He is followed by John McNeill: "The sin remains primarily one of inhospitality."[39] Thus Genesis 19 does not attack homosexuality. The story in Judges 19 is susceptible to the same argument.

In 1 Cor. 6:9 and 1 Tim. 1:10 the words usually thought to point to homosexuals are extremely ambiguous. One word, *malakos*, literally means "soft" and is no technical term for a homosexual. The second, *arsenokoitai*, obviously has sexual connotations. Since, however, the New Testament occurrences are the earliest appearances of the word, it is not easy to be sure what it means. John Boswell in his recent study denies that it refers to a homosexual person in general but rather specifically to the male prostitute, who could serve heterosexual or homosexual clients. At any rate, the sin is prostitution, not homosexuality in itself.[40] If this is so, neither passage condemns homosexuality in general.

It might seem that only a series of verbal pyrotechnics could eliminate the seemingly obvious reference to homosexuality in Romans 1. This has, however, occasionally been attempted. George Edwards in a paper prepared for the UPC Task Force argues forcefully that the statements in 1:26–27 must be seen in light of the larger purpose of Paul in the first two chapters. In Romans 1, Paul describes the fall from true obedience to God and sets out certain sinful consequences of this defection. But then, Paul immediately attacks someone, simply called "the man" with the following words. "Therefore you have no excuse, O man, whoever you are, when you judge another; for in passing judgment upon him you condemn yourself, because you, the judge,

---

38. Bailey, *Homosexuality and the Western Christian Tradition*, p. 8. Italics mine.
39. McNeill, *Church and the Homosexual*, p. 50.
40. John Boswell, *Christianity, Social Tolerance, and Homosexuality* (Chicago: Univ. of Chicago Press, 1980), pp. 107, 341–44.

are doing the very same things" (Rom. 2:1). From the context Edwards argues that this "man" is the prideful Jewish boaster (cf. 2:17) who thinks himself better than the pagan. The intent of Paul in these chapters is to show the Jew that he is on the same level as the Gentile; both are in need of grace.

Edwards summarizes: "Paul has not introduced the material in 1:18–32 to moralize upon the repulsive character of the unenlightened and certainly not to provide a preview of Christian imperatives which formally begin at Romans 12. Paul takes up in this section the altogether familiar outlook of the Jewish alazon [boaster] so that this alazon is set up for the total deflation that follows in Romans 2. Consequently Rom. 1:18–32 is not paranetic [ethical] material at all."[41] Since the purpose is not ethical exhortations, Edwards believes it illegitimate to use the passage to establish Christian objections to homosexuality. "It is insisted that attacks on homophilic behavior based on Rom. 1:26f are hermeneutically unsound."[42]

Boswell comes to the same conclusion. Listing his claims in two propositions perhaps can communicate most clearly his position. (1) "The point of the passage is not to stigmatize sexual behavior of any sort but to condemn the Gentiles for their general infidelity."[43] (2) "What is even more important, the persons Paul condemns are manifestly not homosexual: what he derogates are homosexual acts committed by apparently heterosexual persons."[44] Paul is stigmatizing persons who have gone beyond their own personal nature to commit homosexual acts. But this means they must be by nature heterosexual. Thus Paul does not address the situation of persons who are "by nature" homosexually oriented. This argument depends heavily, of course, on the distinction between inversion and perversion described above.

By these means various scholars have attempted to deny the relevance of some or all of the biblical passages which have been presumed to oppose homosexuality. This is not to say that the scholars I have mentioned would deny the relevance of all of the

---

41. George Edwards, "Romans 1:26–27 and Homosexuality: A Study in Context," "Packet 2" of the UPC General Assembly Mission Council, p. 12.
42. Ibid., pp. 16f.
43. Boswell, *Christianity, Social Tolerance, and Homosexuality*, p. 108.
44. Ibid., p. 109.

passages. My purpose, however, is to show that the scholarly machinery is available for one who would want to eliminate the Bible completely from the current discussion. Perhaps the person who comes closest to using them all is Boswell, as can be seen from two of his claims: "In sum, there is only one place in the writings which eventually become the Christian Bible where homosexual relations per se are clearly prohibited—Leviticus—and the context in which the prohibition occurred rendered it inapplicable to the Christian community, at least as moral law."[45] "The New Testament takes no demonstrable position on homosexuality."[46]

CONCLUSION

The above survey is all too short and dangerously simplistic. Even this, however, shows the complexity of both arguments and conclusions. This is not the place to signal my own agreements and disagreements with the interpretations and arguments. That will become clear later. I have simply wanted to alert the reader, before we plunge into the Greco-Roman cultural ethos, about the ultimate aim of our investigations. What follows is not intended to be a portrait of past times, isolated from our debate today. I want to convince the reader, in fact, that Greco-Roman culture decisively influenced New Testament statements about homosexuality, and that this, in turn, informs us about the appropriate and inappropriate use of such statements in our present confrontation about homosexuality in the church.

45. Ibid., p. 113.
46. Ibid., p. 117.

2
The Cultural Background:
A Male Society with
an Ideal of Male Beauty

PERSPECTIVES

Before beginning the reader needs to be aware of the problems
and perspectives of this study. For one thing, to make generalizations about ancient cultures on the basis of textual evidence alone
is a dangerous intellectual game. In the Greco-Roman world most
texts were written by upper-class males about subjects which were
of interest to them. The selective process, which the ancient historian must accept as a given, is enormous. What is known about
women and the lower classes is filtered through the perspectives
and prejudices of this privileged group.

The study of homosexuality in the Greco-Roman world is a case
in point. We know reasonably well the practices and attitudes of
upper-class males; we know almost nothing about such practices
and attitudes of women and the lower class, except that slaves
were often forced to offer sexual services. Does this mean that homosexuality was primarily an upperclass phenomenon? Such a
conclusion can be drawn,[1] but the very limitation of our evidence
makes the judgment precarious.

Another consideration is the vast cultural differentiations
within Greco-Roman society. Despite the spread of Greek ethos
due to Alexander the Great, there were significant differences

1. See, for instance, R. Flaceliere, *Love in Ancient Greece* (New York: Crown,
1962), p. 62. There is no evidence that adequately supports a conclusion of any
sort. By the nature of the cultural situation, however, I would very much doubt
that pederasty was less practiced among the lower classes than among the upper.
Plutarch hints in one passing remark that he thinks the lower classes have the same
customs (*Whether Beasts are Rational* 990D; Plutarch, vol. XII, LCL), but this hardly
counts as conclusive. In the case of this question I agree with the cautionary judgments of John Boswell, *Christianity, Social Tolerance, and Homosexuality* (Chicago:
Univ. of Chicago Press, 1980), pp. 55–58.

among various cultural units. There was Greek and Roman, Egyptian and Jewish, and even the term "Greek" covers a number of cultural distinctions. It is precariously simplistic to lump all of these together as if all lived the same way and had the same attitudes. In Plato's *Symposium*, for example, Pausanias distinguishes among Greek cities which accept the sexual expression of male friendships, those which hold that to be disgraceful, and Athens which is said (not surprisingly) to have a more noble, *if* more complicated, attitude.[2]

Still another matter to keep in mind is the temporal scope of our period. The evidence we will survey reflects roughly eight centuries (fifth century B.C.E. to third century C.E.) of cultural expression. Did patterns remain the same throughout, or were there developments, changes, swings of the pendulum? My study of the material has led me to the conclusion that in both practices and attitudes, within the class that wrote the texts, there is no significant change reflected temporally or geographically. Consequently, while I shall try to remain sensitive to differences of time and space, some readers may feel that I lump together indiscriminately too diverse materials. In a work as brief as this, however, a different format seemed unnecessarily clumsy. In general it is fair to say that practices and attitudes early texts reflect are also mentioned in later centuries.[3]

The class we know about practiced a very specific form of homosexuality. It is named pederasty, literally the "love of boys." In almost all instances a pederastic friendship was the relationship between a male adult or older youth, and a boy or younger youth. One partner, almost always the older, assumed the role of the active partner; the other, almost always the younger, that of the passive. In later chapters I will describe the practices of and attitudes toward pederasty that existed in Greco-Roman cultures, including Judaism. First, however, it is crucial to see what kind of societal dynamic lay behind pederasty. What kind of culture was it that engendered, permitted, and even extolled the virtues of peder-

2. Plato, *Symposium* 182A–C.
3. Nor am I interested in searching for origins. I use early texts only because they seem to shed light on the general phenomenon. That is, since there was no real change or development, Plato can inform us about the reality of homosexuality in Paul's day.

asty? The single overarching answer to this question is that upper-class public society was in most respects male oriented and male dominated.

EDUCATION

Since each city created its own educational system, it is impossible to think of Greco-Roman education as a monolithic entity. Nevertheless, it seems fair to characterize education throughout this period as essentially male-oriented. In the classical Greek period, while primary schools might see boys and girls studying together, the secondary schools—the gymnasia—were certainly mostly for males. In Sparta, girls did attend the secondary schools, but the training at Sparta seems to have been heavily physical, even for the girls.[4]

The clearest picture is given us of the gymnasium at Athens. In the classical period military training was giving way to athletics, and youths studied music, poetry, and writing. H. I. Marrou concludes: "Such was the old Athenian education—artistic rather than intellectual."[5] In the gymnasium the youths exercised in the nude, the aim being to create a strong and beautiful body.

Nudity, of course, need not provoke sexual excitement, but that it could do so is reflected in Athenian law as described by Aeschines, the fourth-century B.C.E. public orator. The schools are not to be open during hours of darkness, so that darkness may not hide sexual encounters.[6] Older males are not permitted in the school, to lessen the possibility of seduction.[7] The dancing teacher must be over forty years old "in order that he may have reached the most temperate time of life before he comes into contact with your children."[8] The *paidagōgos*, the slave attendant of the youths, one of whose duties was to guard the youth from sex-

4. Cf. H. I. Marrou, *A History of Education in Antiquity* (New York: Sheed and Ward, 1956), p. 23.
5. Ibid., p. 43.
6. Aeschines, *Against Timarchus* 10. The laws cited here may have been added later to the original text. They are consonant, however, with what the speech itself says and thus must be a reasonably accurate reflection of the laws of the time.
7. Ibid., 12.
8. Ibid., 11. The translation cited here and elsewhere is that of Charles Adams, *The Speeches of Aeschines*, LCL (Cambridge, Mass.: Harvard Univ. Press, 1958).

ual advances on the way to and from school, must also be carefully controlled.[9] The sexual possibilities virtually inherent in the gymnasia are indirectly reflected in Alcibiades' narration of his attempts to seduce Socrates. "After that I proposed he should go with me to the trainer's, and I trained [literally to train in the nude] with him, expecting to gain my point there. So he trained and wrestled with me many a time when no one was there."[10] Socrates, of course, is pictured as resisting all advances, but Alcibiades' attempt to use the occasions is clear.

Thus the ethos of the gymnasium is all-male, with the striving toward physical strength and beauty the focus of attention. After finishing the course of study at the gymnasium the Athenian youth served for two years in the army, a situation which could only strengthen his inclinations to view the world as essentially a male reality. Those who wished to continue their education after this would attend private schools, schools of rhetoric or philosophy. If these were not exclusively all-male clubs, they were nearly so. The emergence of women as cynic philosophers seems somewhat exceptional.

True, this sexual exclusiveness appears gradually to have broken down in the later centuries. Marrou comments: "As for the girls, from now on they went to primary and secondary schools just like the boys, and sometimes—and not only in Sparta—to the palestra and gymnasium."[11] Girls even began taking part in games. When the Romans adopted styles of Greek education, they maintained this greater freedom of female participation in the educational process.[12] Roman women were even, on occasion, admitted to the upper literary circles. This apparently happened in

9. Ibid., 10.
10. Plato, *Symposium* 217B–C. The translation cited here and elsewhere, unless otherwise noted, is that of W. R. M. Lamb, *Plato*, Vol. V, LCL (Cambridge, Mass.: Harvard Univ. Press, 1961) .
11. *Education in Antiquity*, p. 103. Cf. also p. 144 and S. Pomeroy, *Goddesses, Whores, Wives, and Slaves: Women in Classical Antiquity* (New York: Schocken Books, 1975), pp. 136f.
12. H. I. Marrou, *Education in Antiquity*, pp. 247, 266f, 274. Also Pomeroy, *Goddesses, Whores, Wives, and Slaves*, pp. 136f, 170. But there are the inevitable qualifications and limitations. "Unlike boys, girls did not study with philosophers or rhetoricians outside the home, for they were married at the age when boys were still involved in their pursuit of higher education. Some women were influenced by an intellectual atmosphere at home" (Pomeroy, p. 170).

sufficiently broad circles so that Juvenal's biting portrait of a female dilettante in matters of the mind would make sense to and bring laughter from his readers.

> But most intolerable of all is the woman who as soon as she has sat down to dinner commends Virgil, pardons the dying Dido, and pits the poets against each other, putting Virgil in the one scale and Homer in the other. The grammarians make way before her; the rhetoricians give in; the whole crowd is silenced: no lawyer, no auctioneer will get a word in, no, nor any other woman; so torrential is her speech that you would think that all the pots and bells were being clashed together. Let no one more blow a trumpet or clash a symbol: one woman will be able to bring succour to the labouring moon.[13]

By the first century c.e., then, significant dents in and exceptions to the earlier all-male exclusiveness in education had happened. How is this change to be evaluated? Does it mean that a Greek or Roman youth's sense of the superiority of the male would be significantly different from that in classical Greece? There is no simple way of answering the question. In most aspects of life, women increasingly began to play a more "public," more visible part. There were important, if occasional, male voices of intercession on behalf of women, as when Plutarch argues for the superiority of marriage over pederastic relationships.[14] Nevertheless, these voices are mostly concessive. One hears them saying, "women are not so bad," or "they do have the potential of becoming respectable companions." The impression is that even these are minority voices. Over against them must be placed the strident voices of misogynous authors, such as we will discuss later.[15] It would be my cautious judgment that nothing had really happened in the educational system to dislodge the centrality of the male and his importance. The "men's club" may have begun to admit women in the side door, but the maleness of the club is not threatened. The educated woman must have been the exception rather than the rule.

<hr>

13. Juvenal, *Satire* VI: lines 434–443. The translation is that of G. G. Ramsay, *Juvenal and Persius*, LCL (Cambridge, Mass.: Harvard Univ. Press, 1961). Cf. also Pomeroy, *Goddesses, Whores, Wives, and Slaves*, pp. 170–72, 149.
14. Plutarch, *Erotikos* 769A.
15. E.g., characters in Pseudo-Lucian, *Erōtes* and Achilles Tatius.

ADULT PUBLIC LIFE

The proof of the conclusion just made lies in the obviousness of the male-dominated public life. By the time of adulthood, sexual segregation was a reality. Even the women who had attended school were now "safely" at home, almost surely married, keeping close to the women's quarters, having as their primary concern the affairs of the household. This is certainly the case in the older period. In a remarkable passage in Xenophon, a character named Ischomachos describes how he has trained his wife and what duties he has assigned her. He never, he claims, spends time indoors at his house, because his wife takes charge completely of what is indoors. In fact, that seems to be the major division of labor and almost the rationale for the marriage itself. He tells her in answer to a question she asks: "Your duty will be to remain indoors and send out those servants whose work is outside, and superintend those who are to work indoors. . . . "[16] Even if highly idealized, the ruling husband and the compliant wife who will do anything to please her husband and who stays out of sight must reflect something of the reality of those classes which could afford such a household with slaves.[17]

Certainly public life was the property of the male. Only males could vote or hold office (apart from certain religious offices).[18] Since only males went to the upper schools which trained one for the professional life, this is only a consequence of educational practices. For most of the period and geography we are considering, a professional male could probably spend his entire day, once he left his house until he returned, without ever having to speak to a woman.

There were, of course, exceptions and local differences. Much has been made of these in recent years. There were women of

16. Xenophon, *Oeconomicus* VII, 35. The translation is that of E. C. Marchant, *Xenophon: Memorabilia and Oeconomicus*, LCL (Cambridge, Mass.: Harvard Univ. Press, 1923).

17. Flaceliere comments: "It should be borne in mind that women were almost entirely excluded from Greek social life, which resembled a man's club," *Love in Ancient Greece*, p. 65.

18. Cf. e.g., the description by S. Heyob of the participation of women as priestesses in the Isis cult: *The Cult of Isis among Women in the Greco-Roman World* (Leiden: E. J. Brill, 1975), pp. 81–110.

power, Hellenistic queens, wives and mothers of the Roman emperors, business women, etc.[19] But in most of these cases, the women exercised their power through their men while, as far as the public was concerned, remaining as hidden as if they had no power at all. Wives of emperors could make and unmake the imperial succession, but they still did not address the Senate.[20] My point is not that no women performed important roles that affected the public life; it is, rather, that when one looked around at the voters, the court cases, the meetings of the city officials, the larger political organizations, the local "city councils," or the Senate of Rome, one would see nothing to suggest that the "men's club" was not in complete control.[21]

In sum, despite the important exceptions, public culture of these centuries was male oriented, and the apposite *intellectual and, indeed, affective partner to a male was another male.*[22] Wives in general had a much lower educational level than did the men. They were not chosen as wives, by and large, for intellectual or romantic reasons; they were not, therefore, sought out as com-

19. Cf. Grace Macurdy, *Hellenistic Queens* (Baltimore: John Hopkins Univ. Press, 1932); Pomeroy, *Goddesses, Whores, Wives, and Slaves*, pp. 120–189.

20. Cf. Pomeroy, *Goddesses, Whores, Wives, and Slaves*, pp. 185–89. "Roman women were given no true political offices and were forced to exert their influence through their men. Unlike Cleopatra, they were the power behind the throne, but the throne could never be theirs, and their interference in politics aroused resentment" (p. 189). Pomeroy does give some examples of Roman women who could, when it seemed necessary, make speeches in public places, notably Hortensia in the Roman forum in 42 B.C.E.; cf. pp. 175–79. These are clearly exceptional.

21. Illustrative of the men's club is the banquet. In Greek culture, at least, women seem to have been completely excluded. The only female present in Plato's *Symposium* is a flute girl, and she is dismissed when the males decide to have serious conversation. Eryximachus says: "I next propose that the flute-girl who came in just now be dismissed: let her pipe to herself or, if she likes, to the womenfolk within, but let us seek our entertainment today in conversation" (176E). This reveals that there are women in the house but they do not presume to enter the room of the banquet. Furthermore, the female is dismissed when the party turns serious, indicating there is no thought that she might contribute to anything but her trade. At Xenophon's *Symposium*, likewise, the only females present are a musician and an acrobat. Petronius portrays a different situation in the famous banquet scene at Trimalchio's house in the *Satyricon*. Here among the many males present there are two wives, Trimalchio's own and one of a guest. As far as I can tell, however, all of the myriads of servants are male.

22. One can, of course, call to mind another famous exception, the occasional female prostitute who had some intellectual gifts and training. These were virtually the only women who were able to become intellectual *and* affective partners with men.

23

panions by their husbands. That males would seek out other males for companionships of various sorts, if there were no taboos in the matter, is not surprising.

THE IDEAL OF BEAUTY

Also crucial to understanding the background of pederasty is the emphasis which Greeks placed upon the ideal of beauty. While we may instinctively think that the Greeks meant beauty of mind, that is a prejudiced view we have inherited from the philosophers. Beauty for the Greek was primarily physical comeliness. As we have seen, athletics formed the center of education. While originally this may have stemmed from the need to produce powerful soldiers, by later times the beautiful boy-form had become an end in itself and the "classical" expression of physical beauty. Ancient pinups were much more likely to be of male figures than of female. And it is crucial to realize that it was the adult male who would have been interested in such pinups.

The primary word to describe such beautiful youths was the Greek adjective, *kalos*. K. J. Dover succinctly describes the meaning of this word. It "means 'beautiful,' 'handsome,' 'pretty,' 'attractive,' or 'lovely' when applied to a human being, animal, object or place. . . . It must be emphasized that the Greeks did not call a person 'beautiful' by virtue of that person's morals, intelligence, ability or temperament, but solely by virtue of shape, colour, texture and movement."[23] Thus when a youth is called *kalos* by his adult admirer, it does not refer to moral, intellectual, or spiritual achievement, but "solely" to his physical properties. Dover has collected the evidence from inscriptions, epigrams, and vase paintings, which copiously use the phrase, "*kalos* is (name)."[24] The person so called could be either male or female (fem. *kalē*), so it is important to note that this data reveals a "great preponderance of male names."[25] Not all of this evidence for the singling out of

---

23. K. J. Dover, *Greek Homosexuality* (Cambridge, Mass.: Harvard Univ. Press, 1978), pp. 15f. Similar judgments by Paul Brandt (pseud. Hans Licht), *Sexual Life in Ancient Greece* (London: George Routledge & Sons, 1932), pp. 418f, and Flaceliere, *Love in Ancient Greece*, p. 65.
24. Dover, *Greek Homosexuality*, pp. 111–22.
25. Ibid., p. 115. Cf. also Brandt, *Sexual Life in Ancient Greece*, pp. 427–30.

beautiful boys suggests pederastic interest. Dover does conclude, however, that one is "justified in treating the quantity of the materials as evidence of Greek male society's preoccupation with the beauty of boys and youths, and the ubiquity of 'boy' and 'girl'— not 'youth,' 'man' or 'woman'—in the formulae reminds us . . . of the characteristic Greek conception of sexuality as a relationship between a senior and a junior partner."[26]

Thus in this all-male society the beauty of the male youth was, perhaps, the key symbol and organizing center for adult male eroticism. Marrou concludes: "'Beautiful'—*kalos*—refers to physical beauty, with the inevitable 'aura' of eroticism that had come to accompany it."[27] This author points to a scene in Plato's *Charmides*, a dialogue named after a beautiful youth. As the youth enters the room, all those present (both young and old) stare at him because of his beauty. Chaerephon asks Socrates if he agrees Charmides has a beautiful face. Socrates agrees, but Chaerephon responds, "Yet if he would consent to strip you would think he had no face, he has such perfect beauty of form" (i.e., his body is even more beautiful than his face).[28] A similar encomium appears in Xenophon's *Symposium*. When the beautiful youth Autolycus, enters the room, it causes all those present (of course mostly only males) to fasten their attention upon him. "A person who took note of the course of events would have come at once to the conclusion that beauty (*to kallos*) is in its essence something regal, especially when, as in the present case of Autolycus, its possessor joins with it modesty and sobriety. For in the first place, just as the sudden glow of a light at night draws all eyes to itself, so now the beauty of Autolycus compelled everyone to look at him. And again, there was not one of the onlookers who did not feel his soul strangely stirred by the boy. . . . "[29]

For our purposes it is important to inquire, if we can obtain the answer, what this ideal of beauty was. What *did* the beautiful

26. Ibid., pp. 121f. So also Brandt, *Sexual Life in Ancient Greece*, pp. 418f.
27. Marrou, *Education in Antiquity*, p. 44.
28. Ibid., p. 44. The text is Plato, *Charmides* 154B–D. The translation is that of W. R. M. Lamb, *Plato*, Vol. 12, LCL (Cambridge, Mass.: Harvard Univ. Press, 1954).
29. Xenophon, *Symposium* 1.8f. The translation here and elsewhere is that of O. J. Todd, *Xenophon: Anabasis, Books IV–VII, Symposium and Apologia*, LCL (Cambridge, Mass.: Harvard Univ. Press, 1932).

youth look like? For an answer we have to rely largely on Greek sculpture and painting. Dover argues that in the earlier period Greek males are characterized by massive features. During this time women seem to be drawn or sculpted in some imitation of the male figure. After the mid-fifth century, however, "it is arguable that . . . men were increasingly assimilated to women."[30] The ideal of the male figure has thus begun to change. In the later period it will reflect the image of the female, slender and sensuous; *it will resemble the bodily contours of the girl.* Perhaps already Aristophanes senses this change in his conservative defense of the old ways in a passage in *The Clouds.*[31] To follow the old ways results in a physique of a shining breast, clear skin, large shoulders, a little tongue, large buttocks, a small penis. The new (and not so good) way will lead to a physique described as a narrow breast, pale skin, narrow shoulders, a huge tongue, skinny buttocks and a large penis. It is particularly the difference in size of shoulders and buttocks which reflects a change in vogue for the "new generation" toward an ideal of male beauty of more slender proportions than once had been the norm.

The sculptures that I know that suggest the best presentation of what the early Hellenistic world began to see as male youthful beauty are first, the sensuous and lithe statue of Hermes by Praxilites (fourth century B.C.E.), and second, the essentially female form (purely apart from the sexual organs) of the hermaphrodite (the male-female in one body), the setting to sculpture of an age-old idea of bisexuality. In a monograph on the hermaphrodite, M. Delcourt also notes the change from archaic to Hellenistic centuries. Originally, for example, Dionysus is portrayed as "bearded and lusty."[32] In later times, however, he is sculpted in the form of "the slender, languid adolescent."[33] This later form "pandered to the Greek taste for adolescent beauty."[34] The same transformation occurred in representations of the hermaphrodite.[35]

30. Dover, *Greek Homosexuality*, p. 71
31. Aristophanes, *The Clouds*, ll. 1009–19.
32. M. Delcourt, *Hermaphrodite* (London: Studio Books, 1961), p. 24.
33. Ibid., p. 27.
34. Ibid.
35. Ibid., p. 38.

Thus increasingly the ideal of youthful male beauty was becoming modeled after that of the young female form. This is entirely consonant with what I shall later describe in detail: the adult male was most attracted to a male youth when the youth was in bodily form most like that of a female. As one third century c.e. writer said: "For even boys are handsome . . . only so long as they look like a woman."[36] Here is the startling irony; the all-male club excluded women only to bring them back as sexual partners in the disguise of the beautiful male youth.

Greco-Roman homosexual culture, it should by now be clear, had a background and a set of patterns completely different from those of our own day. The practices of pederasty emerged out of the dominant social matrix of the day. In some quarters pederastic relations were extolled, in almost all quarters condoned. There was no need to be "in the closet" about homosexual preferences. Thus it is important to keep in mind that Greco-Roman pederasty was practiced by a large number of people in part because it was socially acceptable, while by many people actually idealized as a normal course in the process of maturation. In short the culture we are investigating can fairly be said to be bisexual, since many adult pederasts were or would be married and carry on sexual relationships with both sexes.[37]

The scene in contemporary homosexual culture is often claimed to be different. On the one hand, the "closet" mentality is still very much a part of the ethos today. A person is hardly likely to be enticed to become a homosexual by the dominant strands of our culture. On the other, many male and female homosexuals believe that they have only a single sex preference. This is for them a given, not a socially acquired or socially induced direction. As we have already seen, some authors claim this naturally given sexual inclination to be *inversion*, rather than perversion.[38]

I do not find myself competent to make a judgment about the

---

36. Athenaeus, *Deipnosophists* XIII. 605D. He claims to be citing an earlier source. The translation is that of C. Gulick, *Athenaeus: The Deipnosophists*, Vol. VI, LCL (Cambridge, Mass.: Harvard Univ. Press, 1937).
37. Cf. the discussion about psychological issues in Appendix C.
38. D. S. Bailey, *Homosexuality and the Western Christian Tradition* (New York and London: Longmans, Green & Co., 1955), p. xi and John McNeill, *The Church and the Homosexual* (Kansas City, Kansas: Sheed, Andrews and McMeel, 1976), p. 42.

validity of such a distinction. I simply wish to point out that, given the social context of Greco-Roman homosexuality, it would be impossible to distinguish in that society between a male who was inverted and one who was perverted. If such a distinction is psychologically valid, then doubtlessly both sorts are represented in our texts. Certainly this distinction was unknown to them.[39]

39. Boswell appears to claim the contrary as when, e.g., he writes: "What is even more important, the persons Paul condemns are manifestly not homosexual: what he derogates are homosexual acts committed by apparently heterosexual persons" (*Christianity, Social Tolerance, and Homosexuality*, p. 109). This exegesis of Rom. 1:26–27 seems forced to me.

3
Pederastic Practices

Although the model for male homosexuality in the Greco-Roman world was pederastic, it does not mean that homosexual relationships were all of one sort. Far from it. Pederasty ran from one extreme of an uplifting educational process between youth and adult to the other, sordid extreme of slave prostitution, with several stages in between. We cannot flinch from describing these relationships in detail, however unpleasant this may be to some. As I have said, to understand the New Testament, we need to know just what it was against.

PEDERASTY SUBLIMATED

In most pederastic relationships sexual gratification was given or received. At the same time there is a constant theme throughout ancient literature of a higher, philosophical, sublimated relationship which had education and wisdom, rather than sexual satisfaction, as its goal. The most famous model, of course, for this philosophical ideal is Socrates as portrayed by Plato, hence the term "Platonic" for a sublimated, nonsexualized homosexual relationship. Without doubting the accuracy of this portrait (although some ancient authors did), it is impossible to generalize from one historical example to the popularity and chastity of other relationships based on this or other similar models. For one thing, even Plato acknowledges that some felt it proper to combine the search for wisdom with sexual expression; for another, it was not uncommon for contemporaries of the philosophers to accuse them of using their ideal to cover up actual sexual desires and practices. For our purposes it is adequate to take the philosophers at their word and simply report the ideal relationship as they described it. There will be space later for the rebuttal of the skeptics.

In Sparta, pederasty was closely linked with military training and service. In H. I. Marrou's term it was a "comradeship of warriors."[1] The ideal was for each youth to have an adult lover who would train him in military prowess. In battle they fought side by side. At the same time the presence of the beloved was a spur to valiant action by the adult, who would not want to be shamed in the eyes of his beloved. The memory of this tradition is still alive in the time of Plutarch (first–second century C.E.).[2]

In the Platonic ideal, military education is transformed into the search for wisdom with the adult lover as teacher and model. In the *Symposium* Pausanius makes a distinction between a noble and a base love of boys. The noble sort is interested primarily in educating the youth and proof of this is precisely that the adult chooses a male youth rather than a girl, since the male has "the robuster nature and a larger share of mind."[3] Furthermore this noble love begins only when the youths "begin to acquire some mind—a growth associated with that of down on their chins. . . . For I conceive that those who begin to love them at this age are prepared to be always with them and share all with them as long as life shall last."[4] The context suggests, however, that Pausanius is not denying the possibility of sexual gratification within such an educational model. His argument seems to be that if the emphasis is on wisdom, it is appropriate for sexual encounters also to be a part of the friendship.[5]

For Plato himself, Socrates is the exemplar of this highest love, which fastens intently on wisdom and beauty and is not interested

1. H. I. Marrou, *A History of Education in Antiquity* (New York: Sheed and Ward, 1956), pp. 26f.
2. Plutarch, *Lycurgus* XVIII. 4. Cf. also Plato, *Symposium* 179A; Strabo, *Geography* X. 4.21. Also Marrou, *Education in Antiquity*, p. 28.
3. Plato, *Symposium* 181C. The reader should not think that the views represented by the various speakers in Plato's dialogues are necessarily those of Plato himself. Pausanius no doubt reflects a rather popular, semiphilosophic set of views in Athens, but in this speech he is different in several points from what may be Plato's own judgment, expressed most nearly by Socrates.
4. Ibid., 181D. Pausanias here pictures an ideal of permanency which seems to have been actualized rather infrequently. In the case of Pausanias, whose beloved was Agathon, however, there is some evidence that their friendship lasted for several years at least. Cf. K. J. Dover, *Greek Homosexuality* (Cambridge, Mass.: Harvard Univ. Press, 1978), p. 84.
5. Plato, *Symposium* 184C.

in sexual gratification. The comic, yet moving speech of Alcibiades in the *Symposium* describes with modest openness the handsome youth's attempts to seduce the philosopher, all to no avail.[6] He eventually tricks Socrates into spending the night with him, having wined and dined him, and sleeps together with him under one cloak with arms entwined. But Alcibiades has to concede: "When I arose I had in no more particular sense slept a night with Socrates than if it had been with my father or my elder brother."[7]

This philosophic ideal remained a part of Greco-Roman culture down to the end of the period with which we are concerned. Maximus of Tyre (second century C.E.) defends Platonic love as that which strives for goodness and beauty in contrast to a base and foreign love of pleasure.[8] Later Athenaeus Naucratis (third century C.E.) reports that the Stoics "are always repeating that one should not love bodies but the soul."[9]

Even in this idealization, forms of sexual expression were not always ruled out of court. Legitimate affection could be manifested in kisses and embraces, even if the act of intercourse was prohibited. At Sparta, for example, according to Cicero, a sort of "bundling" was permitted between lover and beloved; they could sleep together if a cloak was placed *between* their bodies.[10] Thus they could embrace and kiss but not consummate the sexual act. Such compromises were, no doubt, further cause for suspicion in the larger culture that followers of this pattern did not always limit themselves to their ideal.

The fact that primarily beautiful youths were sought after would be further cause for doubt. R. Flaceliere wryly comments: "It may well be objected, however, that since not all young Athenians were handsome, the education of the less attractive must have suffered."[11] Furthermore, the frequent assertions that lovers *should* retain permanent relations with the emerging adult

6. Ibid., 217BC.
7. Ibid., 219CD.
8. Maximus of Tyre, *Philosophumena* XIX (89b).
9. Athenaeus, *Deipnosophists* XIII. 563E. The speaker takes these affirmations to be cover-ups for sexual activities, but at least it shows the philosophic ideal still alive. Cf. also Pseudo-Lucian, *Erōtes* 49.
10. Cicero, *De Re Publica* IV. iv (a fragment, given this notation in the LCL edition).
11. R. Flaceliere, *Love in Ancient Greece* (New York: Crown, 1962), pp. 90f.

probably suggests that often the opposite happened—as seems indeed to have been customary in more explicitly sexual relationships.[12] Nevertheless it seems unduly skeptical to doubt that the ideal was often realized. Genuine education must have taken place, and it is not difficult to believe that many such relationships were affectionate without becoming explicitly sexual. Even when there was sexual expression, the primary emphasis may still have been on education.

PEDERASTY AS VOLUNTARY
SEXUAL ENCOUNTER

On the other hand, many boys, youths, and adult males voluntarily entered into a primarily romantic relationship in which the older partner expected to and did receive sexual gratification. The older adult was the active partner, the *erastēs* (lover), usually seeking out the relationship, provoking the sexual contact, and in one way or another obtaining orgasm by the use of the boy's body. The younger person, on the other hand, was the passive partner (at least normally) and was called the beloved, the *erōmenos*. Apparently the beloved did not desire, or at least did not expect, sexual gratification from his older lover. Indeed, according to Dover, if a youth did feel pleasure he was considered no better than a prostitute.[13] At any rate, there is no evidence that he was given an opportunity to be satisfied. His bodily activity was simply to provide sexual satisfaction for his lover.

The age of the younger partner varied, and there is much uncertainty and lack of precision about the evidence. He may be called *pais*, "boy," which might point to an age prior to puberty, or at least not beyond it. He may also be identified as *meirakion*, an older youth past puberty.[14] If it is correct that youths were the more desirable the more they looked like a woman, then the appearance of facial hair could signal the end of the adult's interest

12. In such a case the statements that a person *should* do such and such indicate strongly that many people are *not* doing what the speaker or writer thinks appropriate.

13. Dover, *Greek Homosexuality*, p. 52.

14. Cf. M. H. E. Meier, enlarged by L. R. de Pogey-Castries, *Histoire de l'amour grec dans l'antiquite* (Paris: Stendhal et Compagnie, 1930), pp. 15–17.

in the youth. On the other hand, it is clear that some relationships lasted long after the beginning of puberty (this is the significance of the word *meirakion*). The typical pattern was probably to find a more youthful boy when the present beloved reached clearly into pubertal masculinity.[15] Aeschines, at age 45, claims by that time to have had several beloveds, which suggests a rather rapid rate of turnover.[16] We will discuss in a separate section youths who attempted to prolong their youthful appearances into adulthood so that they could continue, for various reasons, the role of the passive partner.

The age of the older partner also seems to have had great range to it. It has been suggested that when adult males married, they gave up their pederastic friendships.[17] I do not think that this can be substantiated, much less that all such males even married at all.[18] Aeschines is an active lover at 45. Lysias (fifth–fourth century B.C.E.) by his own admission was in his late fifties when such a fierce competition arose between another adult and himself over a beloved that it resulted in altercations and eventually ended in court.[19]

Young men might also begin to assume the active role of lover very soon after giving up the passive role. A few of the vase paint-

15. The texts seem to me clearly to suggest this was the common practice. It is well summed up in a late epigram: "I hate the unkind hair that begins to grow too soon," *Palatine Anthology* V. 277 (Cf. *The Greek Anthology*, LCL). Flaceliere can comment: "As a rule the first signs of down on the chin of the beloved deprived him of his lover. But there were exceptions to this convention," *Love in Ancient Greece*, p. 69. This is very clearly the point of the passage in Plutarch, *Erōtikos* 770BC. "You are well aware, I take it, how often men condemn and make jests about the inconstancy of boy-lovers. They say that such friendships are parted by a hair as eggs are." The translation used here and elsewhere, unless otherwise noted, is that of W. C. Helmbold, *Plutarch: Moralia*, Vol. IX, LCL (Cambridge, Mass.: Harvard Univ. Press, 1961). Exceptions to the general rule are usually noted by the ancients as remarkable. The most famous is the beautiful Agathon, in classical Athens. He was so outstanding even in his bearded stage that Euripides is said to have exclaimed, "For the beautiful even the autumn is beautiful," cited by Plutarch in the passage just referred to. That the bearded Agathon is nevertheless called "autumn" proves the unusualness of that situation. For other exceptions cf. Plato, *Protagoras* 309BC; Plato, *Symposium* 181CD; and *Palatine Anthology* XII. 4.
16. Aeschines, *Timarchus* 136.
17. G. Devereux, "Greek Pseudo-Homosexuality and the 'Greek Miracle,'" *Symbolae Osloenses* 42 (1968): 70, 72; Dover, *Greek Homosexuality*, pp. 171f.
18. There is, however, a suggestion in a poem of Catullus (no. 61) that a bridegroom is prepared to give up his beloved because of his marriage.
19. Lysias, *Against Simon*.

ings collected by Dover suggest sexual activity of near equals in age, and this author points to the occasional use of *neaniskos* ("young man") to denote the older person. He comments: "This suggests the possibility of homosexual relationships between co-evals, perhaps conventionally disguised by the acceptance, on the part of one partner, of the designation *pais; but the vase-paintings do not make much use of such a relationship.*"[20] There are rare textual references to same-age youths in sexual relationships and an early citation in Xenophon to an age reversal in which a beardless youth is the lover (i.e. active partner) of one who is already bearded.[21]

In a complex situation such as this, exceptions to any rule will occur. The following generalizations, however, will be true of the great majority of known instances.

1. In the typical romantic relationship, the beloved is most often a boy or youth around the age of puberty extending at times into the late teens.

2. The lover is most likely to be an adult, probably older than twenty years, the upper age extending indefinitely, at times to middle age and even beyond.

3. There are enough variations of the above to blur the focus of the picture. These may well be exceptions, and are on occasion branded as such by the texts themselves. Historical reality can never be completely captured by generalizations.

4. What *does* seem constant, no matter how much the typical age differential was modified in specific instances, is the acceptance of the roles of active and passive by the partners. Xenophon's example is a classic case. There is a relationship between a beardless youth and a bearded young man. What strikes Xenophon is that the younger is the active, the older, the passive partner. That is, the model of the older active and the youthful passive has become so pervasive that these roles are adopted in all circumstances, even where there is an age reversal. Even when the youths are

20. Dover, *Greek Homosexuality*, p. 86, italics mine. Cf. the plate nos. R27, R59, R196, R223, R243, R851, and R954 in his collection.
21. E.g., Xenophon, *Anabasis* II. vi. 28. Cicero, not exactly a friend of Mark Anthony, attacks him because of his *erōmenos* relation with a youth of similar age (Anthony is about two years younger than the other) in *Philippics* II. 44–45. Cf. also plates R59, R196, R243, R547, R851, and R954 in Dover, *Greek Homosexuality*.

near equals in age, roles, borrowed from the adult-youth model, are adopted which create a relationship of inequality, the active and the passive.

5. Apart from certain exceptions of an adult male prostitute who retains his passive (or perhaps also active) role well into adulthood and thus may service adults his age, *I know of no suggestions in the texts that homosexual relationships existed between same-age adults.*

The basic inequality in the typical age pattern is repeated in the actual sexual relationship. The older, active partner enjoyed orgasm with the youth's body but did not reciprocate. How this orgasm was achieved may have varied. Dover, basing himself primarily on early evidence, particularly fifth-century vase paintings, argues that in proper relationships (i.e., with consenting free males) intercourse was "intercrural," that is "between the thighs." The paintings show the older person facing the younger, embracing him, and, stooping slightly, inserting his penis between the thighs of the youth. Anal intercourse, on the other hand, is that forced on prostitutes, slaves (and women!), and is indicative of an improper relationship and a dominating position taken by the active partner.[22]

If this is true for the early period, it does not seem to hold universally for the later period of our study. Much of the evidence comes from the *Erōtes* of Pseudo-Lucian, a text already referred to. This is, perhaps, the most ribald and frank of the extant ancient Greek texts, but for that reason is more revealing about actual practices than more subtle ones. Throughout this treatise both defenders and detractors of pederasty assume the sexual act is anal in nature.[23]

Although I suspect anal intercourse is more prevalent throughout the centuries than Dover suggests, for our purposes the means by which the adult achieved orgasm is relatively unimportant. What must be emphasized is that the sexual encounter remained one of great inequality. The youth granted the older part-

---

22. Dover, *Greek Homosexuality*, pp. 105f. Indications of pederastic anal intercourse in Greek comedy are, he believes, the result of its basically antipederastic attitude, p. 145.

23. E.g., Pseudo-Lucian, *Erōtes* 17, 27. Cf. also Clement, *Paidagogos* II. 10.86f.

ner his body for sexual satisfaction without receiving similar physical pleasure, and perhaps by enduring pain or discomfort. To Christian ears it is in the strongest way ironic that the technical term for this granting of sexual favor is the noun *charis*, and the verb, *charidesthai*, the Pauline words for *grace*, words which he uses to point to God's gracious giving of salvation through the Christ event. The youth bestows a favor (*charidesthai*) by giving his body for the sexual pleasure of the other.

What did the youth receive in return? He expected to receive gifts of various sorts. The beloved in the novel of Achilles Tatius is given a horse, which will later prove his undoing.[24] Small animals such as hares and birds seem to have been more common.[25] Of course, these were just the exterior arrangements. There would, no doubt, have been also the bestowal of romantic affection, some giving of wisdom and experience on the part of the adult, and whatever honor might attach to being the favorite of that particular man.

Summary. I have not treated the sexual dimensions of this pederastic relationship for purposes of voyeurism or pornography. I have done so for what I consider important reasons, namely to establish clearly what quality of relationship must have resulted from these conditions. On the positive side there were certainly good contributions to the well-being of both. For the older partner there was romantic adventure and sexual gratification. For the youth, in addition to the romance, there was some education, perhaps some pseudoparental relationship, and some gifts and favors.

But it cannot be denied, especially if we view this homosexual culture from today's perspective which emphasizes the importance of equality and mutuality in all relationships, that built into the very structure of the relationship were dynamics which could easily slide into destructive rather than constructive results. First, there was the *inequality*. The older person seemingly selected the partner—although the youth could refuse. The older person must have determined what happened in the relationship. Certainly he was the one who received the sexual gratification. Now it

24. Achilles Tatius, *Leucippe and Clitophon* 1. 7.
25. Cf. Dio Chrysostom, *Discourse* 66:11.

is true that inequality is not always destructive and some very necessary relationships have inequality as part of the structure (e.g., teacher-student). Nevertheless, it does not seem to me that a personal (in distinction from institutional) relationship which touched the depths of emotions and sexuality that pederasty did, could reach the level of mutual caring which our age deems so essential.

Second, there was the *impermanency*. The adults seem mostly to have moved from youth to youth, whenever in their judgment the youth was no longer sufficiently still a desirable sexual object. The youth himself had no choice in the matter. And while he may have been glad for the relationship to end, still a sense of being jilted in favor of a younger or more beautiful youth could easily have been present. Again it needs to be acknowledged that impermanency is not always destructive. Many sorts of friendships end without destructive results. When the adult ended the friendship because of change in the body of the youth, however, hurt must have been frequent. The personhood of the youth is revealed to be secondary to his bodily attractiveness. The same kind of pain occurs, obviously enough, in our heterosexual culture based on the beauty of the woman. In neither case does it seem to me to be helpful to the support and growth of persons.

Finally, there was the potential *humiliation*. For all the idealization that philosophers constructed, this threat would be always present. In a relationship in which the youth knew he was desired because of his sexual attractiveness and in which custom demanded that he sexually satisfy his lover yet not expect to receive any physical satisfaction in return, how could he not often be close to the feeling that he was being abused and dehumanized? This might especially be the case where anal intercourse was the favored form of gratification.

Two texts, widely separated in time, poignantly illustrate contemporary judgments (or remembrances?) of this humiliation. One is from Plato. In the *Phaedrus* Socrates is speaking of the feelings of the beloved in the midst of pederastic intercourse. "But what consolation or what pleasure can he [the lover] give the beloved? Must not this protracted intercourse bring him to the uttermost disgust, as he looks at the old, unlovely face, and other things to match, which it is not pleasant even to hear about, to say nothing of being constantly compelled to come into contact with

them [i.e., physically to have to handle]?"[26] The second is from
Plutarch, four centuries later. "[Young men] not naturally vicious,
who have been lured or forced into yielding and letting themselves be abused, forever after mistrust and hate no one on earth
more than the men who so served them and, if opportunity offers, they take a terrible revenge."[27]

I do not wish to fall into the trap of comparing the best of one
culture with the worst of another. I do not wish to be understood
as stating that such destructive moments happened in this particular sexual culture and in no others. I *do* wish to suggest, however,
that the very structure of pederasty as it was fashioned in the
Greco-Roman world made it especially susceptible to these destructive elements.

SLAVE PROSTITUTION

At the opposite end from the voluntary relations described
above were the various forms of slave prostitution, in which boys
would be forced to provide sexual services for their masters or
masters' friends. These boys would, of course, have become slaves
by means of the usual ways: being born to a slave mother, captured in warfare or by pirates (and then sold), picked up as an
exposed baby while still alive, being sold by one's family.
They would have, furthermore, been placed in various sorts of
situations.

There were brothel houses filled with boys for this purpose, although it is not clear that all brothel prostitutes were slaves.
Aeschines in his prosecution of Timarchus makes several references to such houses (*oikēmata*).[28] According to Diogenes Laertius

---

26. Plato, *Phaedrus* 240DE. The translation is that of H. N. Fowler, *Plato*, Vol. I,
LCL (Cambridge, Mass.: Harvard Univ. Press, 1960).

27. Plutarch, *Erōtikos* 768F. The Greek pronoun at the beginning of the sentence
is vague and *could* refer to what I name below as the "effeminate call-boy." Helmbold, the translator of the LCL edition, is probably correct, however, in giving it a
broader meaning. He is supported here by R. Flaceliere, *Plutarque: Dialogue sur
l'amour* (Paris: Société de'édition les belles lettres, 1952), p. 114: "Quant aux jeunes
gens."

28. Aeschines, *Timarchus* 53, 74, 123f, 188. According to John Boswell there was
a tax on homosexual prostitution also in Rome, *Christianity, Social Tolerance, and
Homosexuality* (Chicago: Univ. of Chicago Press, 1980), p. 70.

(third century C.E.) the Phaedo of Plato's circle was captured as a youth and sold to a brothel house. But Phaedo, having become impressed with Socrates and his philosophy, would "close the door," that is, fake the impression that he was servicing a client, then slip out the window to go to listen to Socrates. The latter was so pleased by Phaedo's devotion to wisdom that he had the youth ransomed.[29]

Some enslaved youths, on the other hand, were household servants, there in part to provide sexual services for master and guests. In the *Satyricon*, Encolpius (the hero, or perhaps antihero) has a youthful male friend (perhaps slave) named Giton, who sexually serves his master. The plot thickens, however, when Encolpius's friend, Ascyltos, tries to steal the slave so that he can use him as Encolpius has.[30] Passing reference is made in Lucian's *Timon* to a clean-shaven "lewd slave" who is rewarded for services performed for his master.[31] Perhaps the most poignant example is given by Seneca. He describes one slave, now an adult, who is a wine-server at banquets, there forced to wear women's clothes, kept beardless by hair removal, "dividing his time between his master's drunkenness and his lust. In the chamber he must be a man (*vir*), at the feast a boy (*puer*)."[32]

Apparently it was not uncommon to castrate such beautiful youths, in order to prolong their youthful appearance and therefore their usefulness for pederastic activities. The most famous case (but thus not the most typical) was Nero's treatment of his favorite boy-slave, Sporus. He had the slave castrated, dressed in women's clothes, given a woman's name, and then married to Nero as his wife.[33] There are references elsewhere to castration of slaves and it may have been more than an occasional occurrence in homes whose masters had predilections for boys.[34] I

29. Diogenes Laertius II. 105. Cf. also Dio Chrysostom, *Discourse* 7:133–39.
30. Petronius, *Satyricon* 11, 79f.
31. Lucian, *Timon* 22. Cf. also by the same author, *Alexander the False Prophet* 5.42.
32. Seneca, *Epistle* XLVII. 7. The translation is that of R. M. Gummere, *Seneca. Ad Lucilium: Epistules Morales*, Vol. 1, LCL (Cambridge, Mass.: Harvard Univ. Press, 1925). Cf. also Seneca, *De Brevitate Vitae* 12.5.
33. Told by Suetonius, *Nero* XXVIII and Dio Chrysostom, *Discourse* 21:6–8.
34. E.g., Dio Chrysostom, *Discourse* 21:4 and 77/78:36; Juvenal, *Satire* X. 295–309; Pseudo-Lucian, *Erōtes* 21.

have no evidence, but many suspicions, about what happened to
boys in brothel houses.

THE EFFEMINATE CALL-BOY

There is a final category of person involved in pederastic practices to which we must pay careful attention. This is so because it
may have been of particular influence on New Testament attitudes toward homosexuality. As we shall see, it was certainly a category that was widely excoriated by Greco-Roman culture itself.
In fact, if this culture was united in judgment about any aspect of
homosexuality it was its universal negative assessment of the effeminate call-boy. I coin this term to compensate for the failure of
the ancients to come up with one of their own (for them these
people were simply prostitutes, *pornoi*).[35] By "call-boy" I mean
they were *free* (i.e., nonslave) youths, or adults, who sold themselves to individuals for purposes of providing sexual gratification. With "effeminate" I use the most common description of
such persons in the texts themselves.

Aeschines' prosecution against Timarchus portrays the accused
as a degenerate and insatiably lustful young man who has prostituted himself over and over again to older male adults. Aeschines'
language is reasonably discreet, but it is hard to doubt that the
means of this gratification is anal intercourse. As already mentioned, Aeschines in this prosecution admits that he himself is a
lover of boys but makes a careful distinction between the higher
and the lower sort of pederasty (a commonplace distinction
among philosophers). "To be in love with those who are beautiful
and chaste (*sōphrōn*) is the experience of a kind-hearted and generous soul; but to hire for money and to indulge in licentiousness
is the act of a man who is wanton and ill-bred."[36] Timarchus, of
course, belongs to the latter category because he deliberately seeks
out relationships in which he offers his body for sexual pleasure

35. The word *kinaidos* is perhaps the closest to a technical term for the Greeks.
Cf. Plato, *Georgias* 494E and Athenaeus, *Deipnosophists* XIII. 565ef. The word does
not frequently appear, however, in the majority of texts I have inspected. The
Latin equivalent was, apparently, *catamitus*.
36. Aeschines, *Timarchus* 137. Cf. also Aristophanes, *The Plutus* 11.153–59, although here the validity of the distinction is called into question (*all* may be prostitutes or *pathicus*).

and receives money for it. In the closing arguments Aeschines refers to certain other men who, he argues, belong to the same category as Timarchus; hence Aeschines gives the clear impression that Timarchus is not a unique case.[37] He is not under compulsion to live this way or to make his money in such a fashion—he *chooses* to do it. This is the great moral turpitude of this kind of prostitute and Aeschines' disdain of it would make no sense in a speech of public prosecution unless he thought he could bring his audience with him into the same indignation. Centuries later Plutarch reflects the same disdain in his judgment: "Therefore placing those enjoying the passive role into the worst category of evil, we do not dispense [to them] any share of belief, respect, or friendship."[38]

Perhaps the most famous case, according to Cicero (not an impartial observer here), is Mark Anthony. It may surprise the modern reader who thinks of Anthony as the great lover of Cleopatra to learn that in his youth Anthony was essentially a male homosexual prostitute. Or at least this was the view held of him not only by Cicero but by a person as distant from the immediate scene as Josephus, the Jewish historian. Cicero accuses Anthony of accepting the passive role, becoming a harlot, being taken into the house of a youth as a mistress, to which youth Anthony is said to function as a wife.[39]

When such youths decided the practice was attractive and remunerative enough, they could essentially make their living this way, often by getting taken into someone's house as a "mistress" for varying periods of time. As they grew older, many of them gave added emphasis to the charge of effeminacy by trying to prolong their youthfulness and at times by imitating the toilette of women. Coiffured and perfumed hair, rouged face, careful removal of body hair, and feminine clothes are often part of the descriptions of such prostitutes.[40]

Thus, in distinction from the "noble" boy or youth who allows

37. Aeschines, *Timarchus* 158f.
38. Plutarch, *Erōtikos* 768E, au. trans.
39. Cicero, *Philippics* II. 44f. Josephus, *Antiquities* XV. 23–30.
40. Cf. e.g., Plato, *Phaedrus* 239C; Aristophanes, *Thesmophoriazusae* 138–52, 191f, 217–19, 257f, 262 (all an exaggerated, slanderous portrayal of the beautiful Agathon); Seneca, *Epistle* XLVII.7; Athenaeus, *Deipnosophists* 565b–f; Philo, *Laws* III. 37–39; Clement of Alexandria, *Paidagōgos* III.3.

sexual favors to his lover, and in sharp distinction from the slave under duress, this category consisted of older free youths who accepted the passive role for money. This is the kind of person Dover is referring to when he says that if a person in the passive role got pleasure from the act "he incurs disapproval as a *pornos* (prostitute) . . . and as perverted."[41] The "lewd slave" referred to above was said to have a shaved face.[42] Athenaeus accuses the (to him) hypocritical Stoics of keeping their youthful favorites shaven.[43] Pitch was so often used for such purposes that there were commercial shops which helped men and women remove unwanted hair by this means.[44] Athenaeus also writes about the use of perfume and women's clothing. If a male uses perfume and dresses in a feminine style he earns the name *kinaidos*, a person who practices the passive role in a pederastic relation.[45] Such youths would let their head hair grow long and would coiffure it in feminine fashion.[46]

Thus such persons were seen as effeminate, having lost their masculinity and having adopted the practices of women, allowing themselves to be used as women. Among several words used to slander such persons was *malakos*, a Greek adjective literally meaning "soft" but metaphorically, "effeminate." It is this word which appears in a list of vices Paul gives in 1 Cor. 6:9–10. In an excursus to chapter 4, I will discuss the meaning of this word and its possible relation to pederasty. In chapter 7 I will argue that the word in Paul's list refers specifically to this category of person, the effeminate call-boy.

CONCLUSION

I have been able to give only a superficial overview of the basic kinds of pederastic practices Paul and other early Christians would have heard about. That Paul would have actually known

41. Dover, *Greek Homosexuality*, p. 52.
42. Lucian, *Timon* 22.
43. Athenaeus, *Deipnosophists* 564f, 565f.
44. Clement of Alexandria, *Paidagōgos* III. 3. 15.3f.
45. Athenaeus, *Deipnosophists* XIII. 565e.
46. E.g., Clement of Alexandria, *Paidagōgos* III. 3. 15.2, 17.3; Pseudo-Phocylides, *Maxims* 210.

people who participated in such relationships is hardly likely. What he "knew" probably originated rather from the rumor mills of the day, particularly perhaps from Jewish suspicions about Gentile activities. Since rumors are often larger than life, it may well be that what Paul "knew" were stories and claims of the more sensationalist sort. Since, however, Greco-Roman authors themselves report sensationalist stories, of which I have described only a bare sampling, I am not suggesting that what Paul "knew" was not at times true. We all tend, however, to judge the whole by that part of it we know, or think we know. Thus, it is not hard to imagine that Paul's basic attitude toward pederasty could have been seriously influenced by passing a few coiffured and perfumed call-boys in the marketplace.

That possibility aside, it is clear that most forms of pederasty had at least the *potential* to create concrete relations that would be destructive and dehumanizing to the participants, particularly the youths. Given this potential and its frequent actualization, that early Christians should repudiate all forms of pederasty is not unduly surprising. For that matter, so also did many Greeks as well. For our purposes, the attitudes toward pederasty expressed in the Greco-Roman world are as important as the practices themselves. To these attitudes we now turn.

4

The Great Debate

Since pederasty was an entrenched part of this culture, we should expect to find many positive attitudes and arguments for it—and this is the case. Yet there were many other people throughout the centuries under investigation who rejected its validity and mounted equally sharp arguments against it. One might name this discussion, with only a little hyperbole, a great debate in which each side affirmed, defended, attacked, ridiculed. In this chapter I lay out both sides of the argument, so that we may better understand how the New Testament judgments might have been informed, not only by knowledge of the practices of pederasty, but also by the judgments expressed, pro and con, by Greco-Roman culture. Later, of course, we must study Jewish attitudes toward pederasty, since Jewish Christians would have responded to Greco-Roman cultural phenomena as Jews. Nevertheless, it must be stressed that Paul and his disciple who wrote 1 Timothy were firmly embedded in Greek culture as well.

Evidence is plentiful. In the later centuries a literary genre even appeared which can legitimately be named "debate literature." These are texts in which the speakers argue with each other about the comparative merits of pederasty and heterosexuality, of the love of boys versus that for women. The three that we mine in this chapter are all later than Paul. Since these debates, however, do little more than collect the arguments found in more scattered form throughout the literature of the entire period, it is both convenient and appropriate to use them as reflections of what Paul's contemporaries must have been thinking and saying.[1] I will, of course, marshal earlier evidence as well.

---

1. The debate is the central focus of two treatises. The more inspired of the two is Plutarch's *Erōtikos*. A number of speakers engage in the good-natured discus-

ARGUMENTS FOR PEDERASTY

1. *Pederasty contributes to the growing wisdom of the youth.* As I have already suggested, this argument includes two different positions. The first believes that wisdom should be nurtured only in a non-sexual Platonic relationship. The second permits sexual gratification if pursuit of wisdom is the central focus. Since the philosophic ideal is often expressed in rather delicate and sophisticated terms, I find it difficult to be sure in some instances into which of the subcategories a specific argument falls.

The purely Platonic position is of course modeled by Socrates himself, who is always engaged solely in the search for truth and in helping others along the same path. Aeschines points to this same kind of friendship when he claims that for a lover to love youths who are beautiful (*kalos*) and chaste (*sōphron*) is "the experience of a kind-hearted and generous soul."[2] Of the youthful beloved he says: "It is an honour to be the object of a pure love."[3] In fact, the older person helps guard the chastity (*sōphrosunē*) of the youth.[4]

Even sharper is the position taken by Protogenes in Plutarch's treatise. In contrast to desire for women, it is (the god) love "that attaches himself to a young and talented soul and through friendship brings it to a state of virtue."[5] Pederasty is "simple and unspoiled. You will see it in the schools of philosophy, or perhaps in the gymnasia and palestrae, searching for young men whom it cheers on with a clear and noble cry to the pursuit of virtue when

---

sion, including Plutarch himself. He, in fact, has the last word and comes to the conclusion that heterosexuality is to be preferred, that women can, in fact, be good companions. Pseudo-Lucian's *Erōtes* (perhaps early fourth century), on the other hand, is more sexually oriented, and its author clearly favors pederasty. The third debate occurs merely as one incident in a romance, or novel, by the late second or third-century author, Achilles Tatius. Here both pederastic and heterosexual couples seem to be equally accepted, and the debate, also carried on with good humor, ends with no one the victor. Since these authors have differing perspectives, it seems fair to conclude that the arguments their characters use on either side of the debate accurately reflect the views of the times. Cf. also John Boswell, *Christianity, Social Tolerance, and Homosexuality* (Chicago: Univ. of Chicago Press, 1980), pp. 85–87.
2. Aeschines, *Timarchus*, 137.
3. Ibid.
4. Ibid., 139.
5. Plutarch, *Erōtikos* 750D.

they are found worthy of its attention."[6] Pausanias in the *Symposium* can stand as a witness to the view that the attainment of wisdom is not antithetical to sexual involvement, if the proper priority is observed. Claiming that his view is that held by Athens, he begins by the traditional separation into two kinds of love, one noble, the other base. The base love desires the body more than the soul. It is this kind that "prompts some to say it is a shame (*aiskros*) to gratify (*charidzesthai*) one's lover."[7] As we have already seen, *charidzesthai* is the technical term denoting the giving of the body for the sexual gratification of the other. Pausanius is suggesting that sexual gratification is shameful *if* it is linked specifically with this base love.

But judgment on sexual gratification is a complex one, he later argues: "It is shameful to gratify an evil [man] in an evil [manner], but it is good [to gratify] a kind [man] in a good [manner]."[8] And even more forthrightly later: "One way remains in our custom whereby a favorite may gratify his lover . . . I mean, in the cause of virtue."[9] Shining through the linguistic subtleties is the strong hint that pederastic love can legitimately be combined with sexual relations.

2. *Pederasty is more masculine than heterosexuality.* Under this heading can be placed a series of statements, ranging from a simple affirmation to sharply expressed misogyny.

Again Pausanius is representative. One characteristic of the base love is that men under its sway love women no less than boys.[10] The noble love, on the other hand, has no part of the female; therefore those under its sway "betake them to the male in fondness for what has the robuster nature (*phusis*) and a larger share of mind."[11] Aristophanes is made to say the same thing in

6. Ibid., 751A. For other examples cf. Pseudo-Lucian, *Erōtes*, 33, 49; Athenaeus, *Deipnosophists* XIII, 563ef; Demosthenes (pseudo?), *Erōtikos*; Plato, *Laws* VIII, 837C.
7. Plato, *Symposium* 182A.
8. Ibid., 183D. Words in brackets are not in the Greek but must be supplied to make proper sense. He thus omits the technical term for sexual gratification in the second half of the sentence, yet grammatically and substantively, the word is implied.
9. Ibid., 184BC. It is, of course, possible that the technical words are here intended to be taken metaphorically. I do not, however, think this likely.
10. Ibid., 181B.
11. Ibid., 181C.

his speech in the same treatise (perhaps unfairly if K. J. Dover's judgment is correct that Greek comedy was "fundamentally heterosexual").[12] Protogones' speech in Plutarch's *Erōtikos* moves in the direction of undisguised misogyny. "Genuine love has no connexion whatsoever with the women's quarters. I deny that it is love that you have felt for women and girls, any more than flies feel love for milk or bees for honey or than caterers and cooks have tender emotions for the calves and fowls they fatten in the dark."[13] Heterosexual love is effeminate (*thēlum*) and bastard and should even be forbidden![14] "But that other lax and housebound love, that spends its time in the bosoms and beds of women, ever pursuing a soft life (*ta malthaka*), enervated amid pleasure devoid of manliness (*anandria*) and friendship and inspiration—it should be proscribed."[15]

Even stronger is the position taken by Callicratidas in Pseudo-Lucian. When this character is first introduced, it is said about him that "his hatred for women made him often curse Prometheus."[16] He lives up to his reputation! "Let women be ciphers and be retained merely for childbearing; but in all else away with them, and may I be rid of them."[17] Then follows a torrential assault which attacks the female with charges of ugliness, artificial adornments and cosmetics, extravagant dress, and suspicious activities (including religious).[18]

In the light of today's prejudices, it may seem strange that pederasts could mount so strong an argument for the superior masculinity of male homosexuality. If we keep in mind, however, the

12. K. J. Dover, *Greek Homosexuality* (Cambridge, Mass.: Harvard Univ. Press, 1978), p. 148. In the famous myth about the splitting of original people, Aristophanes says there were three sorts of original creatures: those who were all female, those all male, and those who partook of a mixed nature. The all-male creatures were the best. They have the most manly nature (*andreiotatoi phusei*), manliness (*andreia*), and virility (*arrenōpia*), 191E–192A.
13. Plutarch, *Erōtikos* 750C.
14. Ibid., 750F.
15. Ibid., 751AB. The Greek words suggest the speaker puts the matter more as wishful thinking than as anticipated legal action!
16. Pseudo-Lucian, *Erōtes* 9. The citation here and elsewhere is by M. D. MacLeod, *Lucian*, Vol. VIII, LCL (Cambridge: Harvard Univ. Press, 1967).
17. Ibid., 38.
18. Ibid., 39–43, 51. Cf. also Achilles Tatius, *Leucippe and Clitophon* I. 8; II. 38.

description of the all-male public culture of the Greco-Roman civilization, it should not really surprise. Public life, which centered in the gymnasia, the forums, and the marketplaces was masculine; masculine love is to be found in that context. Women's life, on the other hand, was in the home, and men thought of them as domestic creatures with the appropriate feminine attitudes, concerns, and dress. To enter the "women's quarters" in search of love is to enter the world of the feminine and therefore is effeminate for a male. The misogyny so sharply expressed has, however, a sinister undertone and seems to me more than just the opposite side of the coin to pederasty. What this might suggest cannot be explored here.

3. *Pederasty is more "according to nature" than heterosexuality.* That pederasty is according to nature (*kata phusin*) is a particularly intriguing argument, since those who attack the custom, including Paul, claim precisely the opposite. This is related, however, to the judgment that pederasty is more masculine. Since the virtue of manliness is the true expression of the nature of the male, any movement toward effeminacy distorts that nature. In effect, to claim that pederasty is more masculine is already to claim it as more according to the nature of the male.

We have already seen Pausanias arguing that males have a "robuster nature," and that Aristophanes is made to echo this with the phrase "most manly nature." Furthermore, according to Aristophanes in the same speech, the persons who stem from the all-male creatures have no interest in marriage because of nature (*phusis*) but only because of custom (*nomos*). Since this creature is the highest and best of the three kinds, the implication is that pederasty represents at least the most superior nature.[19] Callicratidas comes close to claiming the naturalness of pederasty, although he does hedge about using the actual phrase. Pederasty is bred into people from childhood and it is "an ordinance enacted by divine laws" (*theiois nomois*).[20] The pederast in the novel by

19. Plato, *Symposium* 192AB.
20. Pseudo Lucian, *Erōtes* 48. The word *nomos* means two entirely different things in these last two references. In Aristophanes' speech, it refers simply to human custom without any divine sanction. In that of Callicratidas it points to ordinances which have been issued by the divinity and thus have permanent, sacred status. If anything, they are even more primary and eternal than nature.

Achilles Tatius also implies this view by contrasting the guileless-
ness of boys with the artificiality of women. He even says that the
kisses of the boy are of nature (*tēs phuseōs*) rather than of art.[21]

Clearly these arguments are very tentative and weak. This
probably means that they are a counterattack against a prior argument that pederasty is what is contrary to nature. As we will see,
this was the most common attack against it.

Finally, it is instructive to see what was *not* defended. There is
no defense of brothel houses or the use of slaves. There is no attempt to defend the effeminate call-boy or any of the practices
and attitudes associated with that situation. There is no attempt to
defend the common custom of the adult leaving his beloved after
a certain age. Quite to the contrary, defenders of pederasty will
often attack such inconstancy and try to convince the audience
that constancy is indeed possible and desirable in a pederastic relationship. In sum, the positive arguments pass over entirely the
more destructive and dehumanizing aspects of ancient homosexuality. Clearly defense is made only of those aspects of the practices
which might have some claim to broad societal acceptance. The
sordid dimensions remain undefended, as if by not speaking
about them they might somehow not exist.

ARGUMENTS AGAINST PEDERASTY

1. *Laws existed which protected youths against sexual assault and which
placed restrictions on freeborn prostitutes.* We can get some sense of attitudes by inspecting the laws that were passed with regard to certain dimensions of pederasty. Unfortunately the evidence is
scanty and for the Greek period mostly early. Even what is known
about Roman law does not produce clear conclusions.

To begin again with Pausanius. Different cities, he says, have
different laws (or should we translate "customs"?). In regions like
Elis and Boethia pederasty is permitted without any restraint (legally one must presume). In Ionia and Barbarian regions, on the
other hand, it is counted a disgrace (*aiskron*), although he does not
say explicitly that there are legal sanctions against it. Both of these

---

21. Achilles Tatius, *Leucippe and Clitophon* II. 38.

extremes, believes Pausanius, are simplistic, and Athenian law is better, if more complex.[22] The text, however, remains tantalizingly vague as to just what this law actually was. Pausanias says that one reason for the *paidagōgos* (a servant who accompanied boys to and from school) was to prevent encounters between the lovers and their boys, but this was surely not a law but a custom.[23]

Fortunately Aeschines comes to our aid in an important, if limited way. In his speech against Timarchus he calls for the clerk of the trial to read three laws pertaining to the regulation of pederasty. These are highly selective, since they are those laws on the grounds of which he will prosecute his opponent. There may well have been other ordinances he does not call to be quoted. The three do, however, give us some sense of what dangers the general Athenian populace saw and what safeguards they felt necessary.[24] I shall cite them in their entirety.

> The teachers of the boys shall open the school-rooms not earlier than sunrise, and they shall close them before sunset. No person who is older than the boys shall be permitted to enter the room while they are there, unless he be a son of the teacher, a brother, or a daughter's husband. If any one enter in violation of this prohibition, he shall be punished with death. The superintendents of the gymnasia shall under no conditions allow any one who has reached the age of manhood to enter the contests of Hermes together with the boys. A gymnasiarch who does permit this and fails to keep such a person out of the gymnasium, shall be liable to the penalties prescribed for the seduction of free-born youth. Every choregus who is appointed by the people shall be more than forty years of age.[25]

The intent of this law is clear. It is designed to protect boy citizens from any sort of sexual harassment during the school day, or the use of the school premises for such harassment at any time of day or night.

22. Plato, *Symposium* 182A–184C.
23. Ibid., 183CD.
24. According to C. D. Adams, the translator of the LCL edition, the laws "were probably composed by an ancient editor," cf. *Speeches of Aeschines*, p. 12, n. 1. As already suggested, however, the cited laws agree precisely with what Aeschines says in his own speech; thus they must be accurate representations of the actual laws "on the books" in Athens at that time.
25. Aeschines, *Timarchus* 12.

If any Athenian shall outrage a free-born child [*pais*], the parent or guardian of the child shall prosecute him before the Thesmothetae, and shall demand a specific penalty. If the court condemn the accused to death, he shall be delivered to the constables and be put to death the same day. If he be condemned to pay a fine, and be unable to pay the fine immediately, he must pay within eleven days after the trial, and he shall remain in prison until payment is made. The same action shall hold against those who abuse the persons of slaves.[26]

This law is a rape law, designed to protect boys from violence. What is remarkable is that even rape of slaves is prohibited— remarkable since it is clear from other evidence that slaves were used for sexual purposes.

If any Athenian shall have prostituted his person, he shall not be permitted to become one of the nine archons, nor to discharge the office of priest, nor to act as an advocate for the state, nor shall he hold any office whatsoever, at home or abroad, whether filled by lot or by election; he shall not be sent as a herald; he shall not take part in debate, nor be present at the public sacrifices; when the citizens are wearing garlands, he shall wear none; and he shall not enter within the limits of the place that has been purified for the assembling of the people. If any man who has been convicted of prostitution act contrary to these prohibitions, he shall be put to death.[27]

This law prohibits any male prostitute (obviously freeborn) from holding city offices or participating in official civic affairs.[28]

At the same time, Aeschines, as we have seen, points to the existence of male brothel houses without suggesting there were laws prohibiting them from operation;[29] and he himself admits that he has loved many youths, been involved in jealousies about them, and even written love poetry to them.[30] Thus we must cautiously conclude that legal sanctions were directed against child molestation and rape and against the infiltration of the despised effeminate prostitute into the public life of the city. The honorable forms of pederasty, as well as slave prostitution, were not legis-

26. Ibid., 16.
27. Ibid., 21.
28. Cf. also Demosthenes, *Against Androtion* 21–24, 30, 73.
29. Aeschines, *Timarchus* 74, 120, 123, 188.
30. Ibid., 136.

lated against and, if Aeschines' speech is at all reflective of actual practice and laws, accepted as perfectly legal.

John Boswell has collected the evidence for possible Roman legal sanctions against homosexuality and concludes similarly that there were *no* laws condemning homosexuality *as such* until the sixth century C.E.[31] There are a number of cases involving pederastic relationships, but Boswell argues, it seems to me correctly, that the crime is never homosexuality as such.[32] Even the *lex scantinia*, which has been popularly interpreted to prohibit homosexuality is probably no exception. Boswell demonstrates the murky uncertainness of the provisions of this law and shows how precarious it is to link the law with homosexuality as such. His conclusion is worth citing at length.

> Homosexual acts could hardly have been illegal in Augustan Rome, where the government not only taxed homosexual prostitution but accorded boy prostitutes a legal holiday; and it is virtually impossible to imagine any law regulating homosexual activities in the Rome in which Martial wrote: not only does he mention by name numerous prominent citizens having homosexual affairs, often listing their partners, but he frankly admits to engaging in such activities himself.[33]

To this might be added the open pederastic inclinations of many of the early emperors themselves.[34]

Thus what evidence we have suggests that there were no legal sanctions against pederasty per se. Laws were enacted to protect citizens from forceful abuse and sexual harassment. Male prostitution was not illegal, although in Athens, at least, there were attempts to separate a citizen prostitute from public life. Aeschines himself, however, is witness to the fact that these laws were often ignored by the city, since he admits Timarchus has in fact been active in city politics.[35]

2. *Platonic love is a cover-up.* It would seem impossible for the proponents of purely Platonic love not to be distrusted. Our evi-

31. John Boswell, *Christianity, Social Tolerance, and Homosexuality* (Chicago: Univ. of Chicago Press, 1980), pp. 63–71.
32. Cf. Valerius Maximus 6.1.9, 12; Dionysius of Halicarnassus XVI. 4, 5.
33. Boswell, *Christianity, Social Tolerance, and Homosexuality*, p. 70.
34. Ibid., p. 61.
35. Aeschines, *Timarchus* 106.

dence here is from the later period. In the *Erōtikos* Daphnaeus argues that pederasty "denies pleasure; that is because it is ashamed and afraid. It needs a fair pretext for approaching the young and beautiful, so it pretends friendship and virtue. . . . But when night comes and all is quiet, sweet is the harvest when the guard's away."[36] Similarly, a crudely comic pederast in Pseudo-Lucian declares: "But may the airy talkers and those who raise their philosophic brows temple-high and even higher, beguile the ignorant with the speciousness of their solemn phrases. For Socrates was as devoted to love as anyone and Alcibiades, once he had lain down beneath the same mantle with him, did not rise unassailed."[37] Perhaps it is dangerous to conclude too much from such harsh judgments, but it might be that the general culture of late antiquity was not buying anymore the pious statements of the philosophical ideal.

3. *Pederasty is effeminate*. While the proponents of pederasty defended its robust masculinity, its detractors argued exactly the reverse: pederasts are effeminate. This holds true for the youth, less so for the adult, but most especially for the effeminate call-boy. Plato voices this judgment through Socrates in the *Phaedrus*. "He [the adult seeker of pleasure] will plainly court a beloved who is effeminate (*malthakos*), not virile, not brought up in the pure sunshine, but in mingled shade, unused to manly toils and the sweat of exertion, but accustomed to a delicate and unmanly (*anandros*) mode of life."[38] Since the *Symposium* at times argues for the manliness of pederastic relations, it cannot be said for certain whether Plato is expressing his own views here; that it was a common judgment need not be doubted.

His contemporary Aristophanes ridicules the noted dramatist, Agathon, in his play, the *Thesmophoriazusae*. Agathon was a famous and beautiful beloved (Plato acknowledges this in the *Symposium*), even in his adult life. Aristophanes, however, makes him into an effeminate, virtually a transvestite. He dresses like a woman, has women's shoes, wears a hairnet, has a womanly complexion as well

36. Plutarch, *Erōtikos* 752A. Cf. also Pseudo-Lucian, *Erōtes* 24.
37. Pseudo-Lucian, *Erōtes* 54; also 24. Cf. also Athenaeus, *Deipnosophists* XIII. 563e, 564f, 565ef, 602f, and 605d.
38. Plato, *Phaedrus* 239C. For complexion of skin cf. also Aristophanes, *Clouds*, line 1017.

as voice, and carries a razor for shaving his body hair.[39] The comedy is broad and Agathon becomes a victim of heterosexually oriented satire. Whether the historical person was at all like the Aristophanic portrayal is irrelevant at this point. Dover has devoted careful work to Aristophanes' "exploitation of any kind of effeminacy for the purpose of jokes about passive homosexuality," and there is no need to duplicate his study here.[40]

In a later text Daphnaeus, in Plutarch's *Erōtikos*, contrasts union with women with that between males. "But the union with males, either unwillingly with force and plunder, or willingly with weakness (*malakia*) and effeminacy (*thēlutēs*), surrendering themselves, as Plato says, 'to be mounted in the custom of four-footed animals and to be sowed with seed contrary to nature'—this is an entirely ill-favored favor (*charis*), shameful, and contrary to Aphrodite."[41] Here it is presumably anal intercourse which is taken to be effeminate.

Athanaeus, in his *Deipnosophists*, points to the same kind of practices judged effeminate by the above texts. To have one's hair removed by pitch or by shaving implies clearly that the person has pederastic relations.[42] Various sources are cited as suspecting that feminine attire, shaving, and use of perfume point to the effeminate call-boy.[43]

There is no harsher or more vehement attack on effeminate men, to my knowledge, than that by Clement of Alexandria. As a pious Christian one would not expect Clement to remain neutral on the subject of homosexuality. His attack is so extreme, however, and so single-mindedly directed against effeminacy that one suspects his cultural heritage or upbringing has strongly influenced him. Thus it seems fair to enlist him at this point as one more example—albeit extreme—of the cultured despisers of pederasty. The passage (*Paidagōgos* III. 3) is far too long to cite, and I will content myself with giving some of the specific charges and some of the flavor of Clement's venom.

39. Aristophanes, *Thesmophoriazusae*, lines 138–52, 191f, 217–19, 257f, 262.
40. Dover, *Greek Homosexuality*, pp. 135–53. The citation is from p. 145.
41. Plutarch, *Erōtikos* 751DE, au. trans. The reference is to Plato, *Phaedrus* 250E.
42. Athenaeus, *Deipnosophists* XIII. 565b. The text and meaning are not entirely clear.
43. Ibid., 565c–f.

The center of Clement's anger seems to be the practice of men removing all of their hair—beard, pubic, and that on arms or legs. He assaults the professional "pitch-plasterers," who have shops devoted entirely to this activity, and he describes their operations with fine scorn and ridicule.[44] He is nearly equally incensed with the practice of male coiffure. Some of his phrases: they "wear their hair in a disreputable fashion that savors of the brothel," "groom their locks like women," "ladylike combings of their hair." He sums up his vitriol: "Is it not womanish for a man to have his hair combed slick, putting each lock in place before a mirror, and to have himself shaved with a razor, for appearance' sake, to have his chin shaved and the hair plucked out and made completely smooth?"[45]

Clement has no doubt as to the sexual preferences of such men. "Their utter shamelessness in public is a sure proof of their wilful depravity in private. He who disowns his manhood by light of day will, beyond the least shadow of doubt, prove himself a woman at night."[46] He becomes more explicit. "We should call them, not men, but pederasts and effeminate creatures; their voices are unmanly and their clothes are the clothes of women both in texture and color."[47] He seems to see enough of such people in Alexandria that he is fearful they are about ready to take over all of society (along, it must be added, with people practicing heterosexual vices). "But, now, debauched living and indulgence in illicit pleasures have gone to such a limit, and every sort of libertinism has become so rife in the cities, that they have become the norm."[48] The hyperintensity of Clement's fear seems both quite modern and quite atypical of his period. At any rate, he demonstrates that the judgment of effeminacy directed toward styles of dressing, clothes, coiffure, perfume, and the like were still very much a part of Hellenistic culture in the third century c.e.

4. *Pederasty lacks mutuality.* The lack of mutuality embedded in

---

44. Clement, *Paidagōgos* III. 3, 15f. The translation used here and elsewhere is that of Simon P. Wood, *Clement of Alexandria: Christ the Educator* (New York: Fathers of the Church, Inc., 1954), V. 23.
45. Ibid., 3, 17.
46. Ibid., 3, 20.
47. Ibid., 3, 23.
48. Ibid., 3, 21.

the structure of pederasty was not lost to the sight of critics. In the *Phaedrus* three passages are of interest. The first, ascribed to Lysias, simply reports that the adults repent of kindnesses given to their beloveds after desire (*epithumia*) has ceased.[49] The second accuses the active partner of deliberately selecting a beloved who is weaker and inferior to him.[50] The most blunt is a passage cited previously but worth repeating. "But what consolation or what pleasure can he give the beloved? Must not this protracted intercourse bring him to the uttermost disgust, as he looks at the old, unlovely face, and other things to match, which it is not pleasant even to hear about, to say nothing of being constantly compelled to come into contact with them?"[51] Here is the sharpest contrast: the lover has pleasure while the beloved feels disgust. A contemporary of Plato makes the same point in other images. "For a youth [*pais*] does not share in the pleasure of the intercourse as a woman does, but looks on, sober, at another in love's intoxication. Consequently, it need not excite any surprise if contempt for the lover is engendered in him."[52]

Even the somewhat crass text of Pseudo-Lucian is sensitive to the issue, and, in fact, puts the judgment with the greatest clarity of any of our texts.

But why do we not pursue those pleasures that are mutual and bring equal delight to the passive and to the active partners? . . . Now men's intercourse with women involves giving like enjoyment in return. For the two sexes part with pleasure only if they have had an equal effect on each other—unless we ought rather to heed the verdict of Tiresias that the woman's enjoyment is twice as great as the man's. And I think it honourable for men not to wish for a selfish pleasure or to seek to gain some private benefit by receiving from anyone the sum total of enjoyment, but to share what they obtain and to requite like with like. But no one could be so mad as to say this in the case of boys. No, the active lover, according to his view of the matter, departs after having obtained an exquisite pleasure, but the one outraged suffers pain and tears at first . . . but of pleasure he has none at all.[53]

49. Plato, *Phaedrus* 231A.
50. Ibid., 239A.
51. Ibid., 240DE.
52. Xenophon, *Symposium* VIII, 21–22.
53. Pseudo-Lucian, *Erōtes* 27.

This passage summarizes perfectly the sense of inequality which is levied on pederastic relationships, especially that of the sexual act itself. Plutarch thinks that there is so much humiliation in the act that even a youth who voluntarily consents is in effect assaulted and raped. It is indeed not surprising that, as he suggests, such a relationship engenders hostility in the one so used.[54]

5. *Pederastic relationships are impermanent.* As we have seen, pederastic relationships normally did not last long. The opponents of the practice were sensitive to this issue and the charge of inconstancy and the flitting about from one beloved to another meets us rather frequently in the literature. Inconstancy is not unrelated to the lack of mutuality cited above, because it is clear that it is the adult male who, generally, begins the relationship and it is he who terminates it.

The speech by Lysias reported in Plato's *Phaedrus* makes the point early in the treatise. Whenever the adult falls in love with a new beloved, he cares more for the new than the old and is prepared to do evil to the old love.[55] Socrates, in the same treatise, puts the matter more sharply. "And while he [the lover] is in love he is harmful and disagreeable, but when his love has ceased he is thereafter false to him whom he formerly hardly induced to endure his wearisome companionship through the hope of future benefits by making promises with many prayers and oaths."[56]

This judgment continued throughout the period. Plutarch, as he warms to the task of defending heterosexuality, reveals that impermanence is a well-known subject. "You are well aware, I take it, how often men condemn and make jests about the inconstancy of boy-lovers. They say that such friendships are parted by a hair as eggs are; that these lovers are like nomads who pass the spring of the year in regions that are lush and blooming and then decamp as though from a hostile country."[57] He does not deny that some permanent relationships were known to exist but he does summarize: "There are very few examples of a durable rela-

54. Plutarch, *Erōtikos* 768EF.
55. Plato, *Phaedrus* 231C.
56. Ibid., 240E–241A.
57. Plutarch, *Erōtikos* 770B.

tionship among boy-lovers. . . . ."[58] The best evidence of the commonness of this charge is that Plutarch is able to say that it is such a public matter to have become a common joke. The issue for us here is not whether any of these charges were accurate, but rather what was being said and believed in by the culture of the day.

6. *Greediness of the youths.* Another way of attacking pederasty is to accuse it of breeding greediness in youths. Once they become accustomed to receiving gifts they come to expect them, ask, and even demand them. Thus there is a fine line between the willful bestowal of favors and prostitution. This charge is found throughout the period. Nowhere, however, does it appear with greater intensity than in Aeschines' fury against Timarchus. Openly called a prostitute, he is accused of selling himself to one man after another, leaving one when another offered him a higher price. The smearing attack makes it very clear that Timarchus not only desires to be used and kept but that he does it for the money he receives.[59]

7. *Jealousy in the lover.* An even stronger attack is directed against degenerate habits in the lover. He becomes, or so it is argued, excessively jealous of the youth's friendships with other adults and makes an attempt to keep the beloved solely for himself. It no longer surprises that an extreme example can be found in the speech of Aeschines. Timarchus has so debased himself that he has sold himself to a wealthy public slave, Pittalacus, who was something of a professional gambler. An even wealthier man, Hegesandrus, talks Timarchus into living with him instead. Pittalacus, enraged, keeps coming to Hegesandrus's house to try to get his beloved back. To stop this, one night Hegesandrus, Timarchus, and some friends invade Pittalacus's house, destroy his gambling devices, tie him to a post, and beat him severely.[60]

---

58. Plutarch, *Erōtikos* 770C. The translation, "Examples of a durable relationship," depends on one Greek word, *sudzugia*, which means literally "yoked together." That is, the idea of "durable" is reading into the context. It is doubtlessly correct reading, but it does go beyond any sort of literal translation. Cf. also Pseudo-Lucian, *Erōtes* 25f; Athenaeus, *Deipnosophists* XIII. 605d; *Palatine Anthology* V. 277.

59. Aeschines, *Timarchus* 40–65. For examples reported by late authors cf. Athenaeus, *Deipnosophists* XIII. 604de, concerning Sophocles; Plutarch, *Erōtikos* 762C for an incident involving Alcibiades.

60. Aeschines, *Timarchus* 54–59.

Pittalacus will later have his revenge. The point is that men seemed quite free to express their jealousy in the most violent of ways. Presumably this story is true, since it occurs in a trial speech and since Aeschines asks for affadavits from people connected with the events.[61]

What is even more interesting in establishing the reality of such extremes is that Aeschines admits that he also knows what it is to act out of jealousy. To ward off his own accusers (in this case Demosthenes), he prepares the hearers for the accusation to come that Aeschines himself has been involved in quarrels and physical fights because of his own pederasty.[62] To this he admits: "I do not deny that I myself have been a lover to this day [he is forty-five], nor do I deny that the jealousies and quarrels that *commonly arise* from the practice have happened in my case."[63] We thus learn from this admission that accusations of jealousy were not simply prejudiced judgments (although they doubtlessly were at times), but fact.

I do not myself know of an example of such accusations from later texts. That it does not reappear in Pseudo-Lucian or Plutarch is surprising; yet it is hard to doubt that such feelings of servitude were as real in the later centuries as in the former. Certainly the whole plot of the *Satyricon* is based on the competition between Enclpius and Ascyltos for the youth Giton. And the pseudo-Plutarchian treatise, *Love Stories*, contains examples of violence done to youths by the adult when the youth could not be persuaded to yield.[64]

8. *Pederasty is contrary to nature* (*para phusin*). Of all accusations against pederasty the most common is that it is contrary to nature, and I can only cite a few examples. While most of the texts are later rather than earlier, the judgment already seems common by the time of Plato. The philosopher himself contrasts heterosexuality with homosexuality. "When male unites with female for procreation, the pleasure experienced is held to be due to nature

61. Cf. a similar altercation, reported in trial, which is the theme of the treatise of Lysias, *Against Simon*.

62. Aeschines, *Timarchus* 135.

63. Ibid., 136, italics mine. For other examples cf. Plato, *Phaedrus* 232C, 239B, 240CD; Xenophon, *Symposium* iv. 52–54.

64. Pseudo-Plutarch, *Love Stories* 772EF, 773F–774A.

(*kata phusin*), but contrary to nature (*para phusin*) when male mates with male or female with female."[65] According to Daphnaeus in *Erōtikos*, pederasty is a "union contrary to nature" (*he para phusin omilia*), in contrast to the natural heterosexual relationship.[66] In Plutarch's humorous treatise, *Whether Beasts are Rational*, Odysseus is attempting to persuade one of his former men, Gryllus, whom Circe turned into a pig, to return to human existence. Gryllus refuses, saying that animals have a better life than humans. It is a life according to nature while humans have distorted and confounded nature. One example Gryllus gives is the natural sexual intercourse of animals in comparison with that of humans. Since animals are wholly concerned with nature (again *phusis*), "Until now the desires of animals have involved intercourse neither of male with male nor of female with female."[67] He concludes that "even men themselves acknowledge that beasts have a better claim to temperance and the non-violation of nature in their pleasures."[68]

Attack on pederasty as *para phusin* is continued in Athenaeus. The story is told of Diogenes who, encountering an effeminate man with shaven chin, asked the man if he had found fault with nature for making him a man rather than a woman.[69] And later a speaker verbally assaults pederastic philosophers: "So, beware, you philosophers who indulge in passion contrary to nature (*para phusin*) who sin against the goddess of love . . . "[70]

It can thus be seen that the use by Paul of *para phusin* in Rom. 1:26–27 is the most common stereotype of Greco-Roman attitudes. For those who opposed pederasty, that which seemed most abhorrent about it was that it violated the natural order of creation, however creation was understood.

---

65. Plato, *Laws* I. 636C; cf. also VIII. 836CD.

66. Plutarch, *Erōtikos* 751C; cf. also 751DE. So also Dionysius of Halicarnassus XVI, 4.

67. Plutarch, *Whether Beasts are Rational* 990D, au. trans. Cf. also Pseudo-Lucian, *Erōtes* 22.

68. Plutarch, *Whether Beasts are Rational* 990EF. The translation here is that of W. C. Helmbold, *Plutarch's Moralia*, Vol. XII, LCL (Cambridge, Mass.: Harvard Univ. Press, 1957).

69. Athenaeus, *Deipnosophists* XIII, 565c.

70. Ibid., 605d. Other examples in Pseudo-Phocylides, *Maxims* 190f; Clement, *Paidagōgos* III. 3, 21, 2.

9. *Women provide superior possibilities than boys.* Given the all-male public society, it is not surprising that the argument that women can be better partners than boys is not a theme carried out with much conviction or dignity. The general range of arguments runs from the crude to the pragmatic. The crude usually concerns the sexual abilities of the woman. She has two orifices instead of one.[71] She is a better lover than the boy, who is unlearned in the sexual art.[72] The pragmatic includes such comments as the longer lasting beauty of the woman over against the youth.[73] And Pseudo-Lucian, as already shown, rises to an unusual level when he makes a strong argument for the need for mutuality in human relationships, a mutuality possible with a woman, not possible with a youth, although even here only the sexual relation seems to be in his mind.[74]

It remains for Plutarch to make the point that even women can be human and provide a mutuality of companionship that makes the heterosexual relationship more than sexual.[75] Certainly Plutarch was of an enlightened stature not reached by many men of his period; yet perhaps even he sounds a bit unconvinced by his own arguments. At least he has a sensitivity to the need for giving in the marriage relationship that strikes me as rare, certainly for his day. In a sentence consonant with Christian attitudes (and quite similar to Paul's attitude, though better put), he writes: "To love in marriage is a greater good than to be loved."[76]

He concludes: "There can be no greater pleasures derived from others nor more continuous services conferred on others than those found in marriage, nor can the beauty of another friendship be so highly esteemed or so enviable as [quoting Homer] when a man and wife keep house in perfect harmony."[77] Alas, this is a lonely voice in his time. As compared with the other texts we have reported, his sensitivity to the humanity of wom-

71. Pseudo-Lucian, *Erōtes* 27.
72. Achilles Tatius, *Leucippe and Clitophon* II. 37.
73. E.g., *Palatine Anthology* V. 277.
74. Pseudo-Lucian, *Erōtes* 27.
75. Plutarch, *Erōtikos*, beginning at 767D.
76. Plutarch, *Erōtikos* 769D, au. trans.
77. Ibid., 770A.

en is atypical, even among those who despised the practice of pederasty.

CONCLUSION

This, then, was the great debate. Strong and sometimes strident voices from the past engaged the other in argument over a widespread and condoned set of customs. In general the debate seems to have been conducted with civility and mutual respect, mostly without acrimony, contrary to today. There seems to have been more emphasis upon "I'm right" and less upon "you're wrong." The debate was conducted with a surprising rationality, given the strong, if often concealed, emotional cathexis of sexual energy. The various arguments from nature do not seem to have an overloaded moral freight, and even the rare appeals to the divine appear to be more literary than religious.

From our perspective the practices of pederasty in the ancient world do raise serious moral questions, questions of denigration and dehumanization of the boys—issues which were discussed in the debate. Yet I do not sense any *homophobia* in the texts under discussion, although there is plenty of *misogyny*. The great debate was between men who disagreed with each other but who were rational enough not to try to legislate the other out of existence.

EXCURSUS:
THE STATUS OF MALAKOS, MALAKIA,
AND MALTHAKOS

Crucial to our understanding of a passage in 1 Corinthians is the meaning of a word, in its various spellings, which has occurred in several texts inspected in this chapter. Among a long list of activities which are said to exclude one from the kingdom of God in 1 Cor. 6:9–10 is the plural adjective, *malakoi*, used as a noun. The word literally means "soft" and can be applied to material like cloth, as in Matt. 11:8: "Why then did you go out? To see a man clothed in soft raiment? Behold, those who wear soft raiment are in kings' houses." Metaphorically, it can then take on a meaning somewhat similar to the English word "soft." A "soft" person is one who does not keep in shape, who needs exercise. In the Greek of the period we are investigating the word is frequently used with the meaning "effeminate." As such it has appeared in several of the texts we have cited, and I have noted its occurrences.

It is at this point that the question arises, what *could* Paul have understood the adjective to mean in the list? Discussion of that must remain until the appropriate place, but a preliminary question needs to be asked at this point. What are the *possible* meanings the word could have in Greek culture, from which the meaning to be given to its use in 1 Corinthians *must* be taken? We cannot assign a meaning to Paul's vocabulary which was not current in the Greek of his day.

Since a literal meaning makes no sense in Paul's case, we must focus attention on the nuances of the metaphorical use or uses. One could simply translate it "effeminate," understanding the reference to be to a man (the ending is masculine) whose life style, in some way, is thought to resemble that of a woman. This was the meaning, in fact, chosen by the King James translators. Two considerations, however, have made that suggestion seem implausible to the majority of interpreters. (1) Following *malakos* in the list is the rare word *arsenokoitēs*, which seems to mean literally "one who has intercourse with males," or at least this is the way it has traditionally been taken.[78] The conjunction of these two words seems to force some sort of connection between *malakoi* and homosexuality, such that some recent translations have given just one English word or phrase for the two Greek words ("homosexual perversion" in New English Bible; "homosexuals" in the first edition of the Revised Standard Version (1946), "sexual perverts" in the second edition (1971). (2) Would Paul be against effeminacy, if it did not connote to him some sort of sexual impropriety? Although I do not think the answer to this is as simple as some people think, most interpreters assume a negative answer to that question and thus conclude that a link has to be made with homosexuality. What light, however, do our texts shed on whether that is a *possible* linkage, that is, whether in the culture of Paul's day the word could carry such a specific and popularly accepted connotation?

The quick and demonstrable answer is that the texts are ambiguous. This ambiguity is clearly seen in a comment by an author of the first century B.C.E., Dionysius of Halicarnassus. Speaking of a ruler, Aristodemas, who had been given the nickname *Malakos*, he expresses uncertainty as to the cause of the name; it was given "either because he became effeminate (*thēludria*) as a child and experienced things suitable to women, as some narrate, or because he was gentle by nature and *malakos* toward anger, as others write."[79] This uncertainty means that *malakos* was *not* a technical term referring to pederasty, but could refer to a quality of life style which *some* people associated with pederastic practices. The word as a nickname appears again, this time in a papyrus letter. The letter refers to one

78. Boswell, *Christianity, Social Tolerance, and Homosexuality*, takes strong exception to this common interpretation, pp. 341–53.
79. Dionysius of Halicarnassus, *Roman Antiquities* VII. 2, 4.

Zenobios the *Malakos*, who is a musician. Nothing in the brief letter makes any suggestion of pederasty.[80]

Dio Chrysostom (first century C.E.) implies even more clearly that the word is not a technical term. People always misjudge others, Dio complains. If one likes to study, that person is branded simple-minded and *malakos*. The context makes no hint of this being a charge of pederasty.[81]

On the other hand, the seemingly inevitable connection with effeminacy and the general practice of pederasty creates definite links between the word and the practice. Two instances from Plutarch which I have not cited before indicate this. The Romans, he writes, think nothing has contributed more to Greek enslavement and *malakia* [the noun] than the gymnasium and its activities, which, he says, include the love of boys (*paiderastein*).[82] While *malakia* is here a general term including far more than pederasty, it does specifically include it. Even more specific is the note of a charge by Gaius Gracchus against a person reviled with *malakia*.[83] Here the context makes it clear the person is accused of pederasty.

To these texts must be added passages already cited. Socrates thinks the base pederastic love seeks a person who is *malthakon*.[84] And the speaker in the *Erōtikos* speaks of the willing youth consenting to pederastic intercourse as one who acts with *malakia*.[85]

Although I do not claim the evidence has been exhausted, I do think what has been presented is clear enough to draw the following conclusions. One, *malakos* or *malakia* is not a technical term to describe people or practices that are pederastic. There *are* technical terms, as we have seen. The lover (*erastēs*), the beloved (*erōmenos, paidika*), to give the body for purposes of intercourse (*charidzesthai, charis*)—all these are ever-present in the literature. In addition to these are certain slang terms, which we have not noted. Even the literal "love of boys" (*paiderasteia*) is common enough. *Malakos* or *malakia* do not in any way have the same status as those technical words. For example, if someone had been nicknamed

80. Hibbeh Papyrus I. 54, 11.

81. Dio Chrysostom, *Discourse* 66:25. Similarly vague and thus not to be specifically associated with pederasty is the use by Xenophon as he writes Socrates' defense statement before the Athenian judges. "So you tell us whether you know of any one who under my influence has fallen from piety into impiety, or from sober into wanton conduct, or from moderation in living into extravagance, or from temperate drinking into sottishness, or from strenuousness into *malakos*, or has been overcome of any other base pleasure," *Apology* 19. The translation is that of O. J. Todd, *Xenophon: Anabasis Books IV–VII and Symposium and Apology*, LCL (Cambridge, Mass.: Harvard Univ. Press, 1932).

82. Plutarch, *Roman Questions* 40.

83. Plutarch, *Gaius Gracchus* IV. 3f.

84. Plato, *Phaedrus* 239C. According to Liddell-Scott-Jones, this is mainly a poetic spelling of *malakos*. The same word is used disparagingly of a heterosexual lover in Plutarch, *Erōtikos* 751B.

85. Plutarch, *Erōtikos* 751D.

"the lover" (erastēs), or "lover of boys" (*paiderastēs*), no one could doubt the meaning of that name, as Dionysius could doubt that of the nickname *malakos.* ·

Two, through the linkage of the metaphorical meaning of "effeminacy," however, *malakos* is used to point in a negative way to people who engage in pederasty—not with great frequency, but often enough for it to be clear this was a convention. While the specific word is not frequent in texts which denounce the free prostitute, the general charge of effeminacy is a common pejorative. Thus the use of *malakos* would almost certainly conjure up images of the effeminate call-boy, *if* the context otherwise suggested some form of pederasty.

5

Palestinian Judaism: Stern Opposition

By this time the reader has a clear picture of Greco-Roman homosexuality and that culture's attitudes toward it. We are thus halfway toward our goal of understanding New Testament reactions to this part of its cultural surroundings. Before we approach the New Testament itself, however, it is necessary to look carefully at a second cultural phenomenon which can only have strongly influenced the positions taken by the early church. This phenomenon is, of course, biblical and postbiblical Judaism in both its Palestinian and Hellenistic forms.

Of the three explicit New Testament passages which mention homosexuality, two are from the pen of Paul, who in both cases seems dependent upon Jewish-influenced tradition, either directly or through Hellenistic Jewish Christianity. Whether the author of the third (1 Timothy) was Jewish cannot be determined.[1] Certainly, however, by the time he wrote, the Greek translation of the Hebrew Bible was basic to the ethical and intellectual life of the churches. Furthermore, Paul himself strode boldly across both Palestinian and Hellenistic Jewish cultures. Whether or not he ever studied with Gamaliel, as Acts claims, his writings reveal such mastery of the exegetical skills of the emerging rabbinic scholarship that he must have been expertly trained in these skills by someone or some school. It is equally clear that he is informed by Hellenistic Judaism. If the author of 1 Timothy was Jewish, he was a Hellenistic Jew.

1. I follow commonly accepted scholarly judgment that 1 and 2 Timothy, along with Titus, were written sometime after Paul's life, perhaps toward the beginning of the second century C.E.

We now know that the male homosexuality Paul knew about and opposed had to have been one or more forms of pederasty. We also know that many Gentiles opposed all of these forms. As we shall see, New Testament opposition to pederasty is expressed in part in terms similar to those used in Greco-Roman culture. The question that now confronts us is the following: Can we understand Paul and 1 Timothy purely from within the confines of the Greco-Roman debate, or did Jewish attitudes also inform the New Testament judgments? To answer this question we must study the Judaism contemporary to the early church. Such a study has to include, although it complicates our work, the Judaism of both rabbinic Palestine and Hellenistic Diaspora.

THE RELIGIOUS EXPRESSIONS
OF PALESTINIAN AND
HELLENISTIC JUDAISM

These two Jewish cultures, of course, held much in common, largely due to the common heritage of the Torah. The Bible provided the *constitution* for all Jewish civilizations and both Hellenistic and Palestinian Judaism took this constitution seriously. Yet any constitution must be interpreted, and it is not surprising that these two forms of Judaism proceeded to interpret the Bible in often similar, often divergent fashions.

What were the basic literary expressions of these Jews? As is to be expected, the *first* was the translation of the Bible into the local language. For the Palestinian Jew this meant Aramaic, and such translations are called *targums*. For the Hellenistic Jew, it meant Greek, a translation which came to be named the Septuagint (LXX). As is inevitable, these translations, just as is the case with any translation, were in part also interpretations. That is, the constitution in being expressed in the language of a particular culture becomes inflected toward the perspectives and needs of that culture. Thus by studying the translations we can learn how the Torah was being interpreted in the postbiblical period. The *second* kind of expression was interpretations and analyses of this constitution. That is, the laws had to be explained; the stories expounded in such a way as to be exciting and meaningful for the present day; cultural manifestations both within and without Judaism explored on the basis of the constitution.

Each culture carried out this second level of expression in different ways and forms. In Palestinian Judaism this second level is extant to us largely through the immense and complicated corpus of legal and theological traditions, loosely called rabbinic literature. The biblical *laws* are here defined, refined, expanded, occasionally contracted. A whole legal system is built up, sometimes directly dependent on, sometimes seemingly independent of, the Bible itself. But the biblical *narratives* are not neglected either. They may be told, alluded to, even occasionally made the basis for legal decisions. What we might call theology, moral teachings, parables, and illustrative examples from the present are also interwoven into the legal corpus.

In Hellenistic Judaism the literary expressions of this second level are quite different in form. While Palestinian Judaism built up its traditions through an accumulation of individual judgments and sayings by a vast number of scholars, what we know of Hellenistic Judaism is limited to a few authors who wrote entire tracts or books. We know this culture largely, though not exclusively, through Philo, an Alexandrian theologian, and Josephus, an apologist and historian of the Jewish people. Neither Philo nor Josephus ignore the legal sections of the Torah. Nevertheless, they do not pay much attention to the current interpretation of the laws. Philo is striving to relate and integrate Greek philosophic traditions with Jewish piety; Josephus, to explain the history of his people, both ancient and contemporary, to what is probably primarily a non-Jewish audience after the debacle of the Jewish revolt against Rome in 66–70 C.E. Thus Philo writes theological treatises of various sorts, almost always, of course, in relation to the Bible. Josephus writes books of history, including his telling of the biblical narrative. A graph will perhaps help the reader understand this rather complicated process. Rabbinic discussions continued far beyond the period of our interest (indeed, they continue today). I will limit our investigation of Palestinian Judaism, however, to the first two centuries of the common era, since the literature itself provides that as a convenient point of

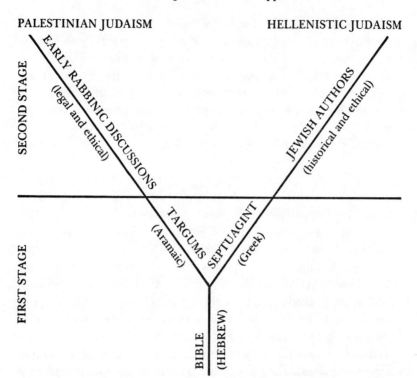

PALESTINIAN JUDAISM   HELLENISTIC JUDAISM

SECOND STAGE

EARLY RABBINIC DISCUSSIONS
(legal and ethical)

JEWISH AUTHORS
(historical and ethical)

FIRST STAGE

TARGUMS
(Aramaic)

SEPTUAGINT
(Greek)

BIBLE
(HEBREW)

closure.[2] Our study of Hellenistic Judaism is forced to an earlier cutoff, for by the beginning of the second century, our two major witnesses are dead.

In this chapter I shall explore Palestinian Judaism, reserving

2. The scholar will recognize that the closure I speak of is the end of the Tannaitic period. I do not include any materials from the later, Amoraic period, except when specifically noted. This is aimed at avoiding as rigidly as possible the kind of technical discussion and terminology which can only confuse the general reader. When I use the phrase "early rabbi," I am *always* referring to a Tannaitic scholar or tradition; when "later rabbi," I am *always* referring to one associated with the Amoraic period. I make no further temporal distinctions. Whether these traditional assignations are historically accurate is an important question but cannot be raised here. My aim is to communicate a general impression of early Jewish attitudes, not to describe historical development (which mostly seems to be lacking anyway). From a scholarly perspective I recognize the inadequacies and awkwardness of this approach, but to keep to my goal of informing the general reader, I could not adopt a more precise organization. The literature used here for the Tannaitic times includes *Mishnah, Tosephta, Siphra*, materials from the *gemara* identified as *baraithas, Midrash Rabbah*, and one passage from *Ben Sirach* for which the original Hebrew text is extant. I am indebted to Paul Billerbeck, *Kommentar zum Neuen Testament aus Talmud und Midrasch*, vol. 3 (Munich: C. L. Beck'sche, 1926), (pp. 68–73, for identification of most of these traditions.

Hellenistic Judaism for the following chapter.[3] First, however, it
is necessary to review briefly the relevant passages in the Torah itself. In chapter 1, I have already pointed to most of them. No
more than there is it my concern here to study these texts in detail. There have been many recent investigations of biblical passages which concern homosexuality, and the interested reader can
consult them.[4] My discussion is designed primarily to lay the
foundation for postbiblical interpretations.

THE TORAH

The first immediate impression of the Hebrew Bible, in comparison with the Greco-Roman literature we have been studying,
is its almost complete silence, perhaps indifference, about homosexuality. Nothing is said about female homosexuality at all, and
the assembled texts of all possible references to male homosexuality make short reading indeed. The reason for this indifference is
usually seen to lie in the absence of homosexuality within ancient
Israel, a judgment that is probably correct.

1. *The Legal Traditions. If* Deut. 23:17–18 should refer to some
form of homosexuality, this would be the earliest law mentioning
homosexuality to achieve definitive status in Israel.[5] "There shall
be no cult prostitute of the daughters of Israel, neither shall there
be a cult prostitute of the sons of Israel. You shall not bring the

3. As all know, the day when these two cultures could be viewed as separate, wa-
tertight compartments is long past. No one doubts anymore the interpenetration
of Hellenism and Judaism, whether in Palestine or in the Diaspora. Nevertheless,
it is pragmatically helpful for our purposes to keep the literature separate.

4. E.g., John McNeill, *The Church and the Homosexual* (Kansas City, Kansas: Sheed
Andrews and McMeel, 1976) pp. 37–87; Tom Horner, *Jonathan Loved David: Homosexuality in Biblical Times* (Philadelphia: Westminster Press, 1978); John Boswell,
Christianity Social Tolerance, and Homosexuality (Chicago: Univ. of Chicago Press,
1980) pp. 91–117, and the ecclesiastical interpretations noted in chapter 1. The
reader can also consult the standard commentaries.

5. The book of Deuteronomy is usually considered that law code established
during Josiah's reform in 621 B.C.E. (cf. 2 Kings 22:1—23:25). Of course the individual laws here as well as in other legal sections of the Pentateuch may antedate
this reform. It is not clear, however, that any of them had been codified into a single manuscript or that before this reform any of them had the support of the royal
court. Thus the effectiveness of the law in Deut. 23:17–18 only begins with the acceptance of the law code in 621 B.C.E. The scholar should note that in the original
text the verses are 18–19.

hire of a harlot, or the wages of a dog, into the house of the Lord your God in payment for any vow; for both of these are an abomination of the Lord your God."[6]

Assuming that the translation, "cult prostitute," is correct, the issue for us is whether the male prostitutes performed sexual services for other males. This is sometimes asserted.[7] If that were so, however, how could such homosexual acts function even symbolically in a cult invaded by these fertility activities? It is more plausible that the acts were heterosexual, suggesting and symbolizing the power over the female womb which the deity was believed to have.[8] Even if male prostitutes were performing homosexual acts, the passage in Deuteronomy is so clearly oriented to stamping out a specific *cultic* practice that the law cannot in any way be considered a general indictment of homosexuality.[9] The text, however, is important, because some postbiblical traditions will read it as referring to secular male prostitution. We will discuss this interpretation below.

Only with the codification of the Priestly code in the fifth–

6. The Hebrew words which lie behind the translation, "cult prostitute," appear only infrequently in the Bible and must point to some cultic functionary taken over into the religion of Israel from Canaanite fertility religion. This person is almost certainly a sacral prostitute; Gen. 38:13–24 specifically links the word to prostitution, and Hos. 4:14, with the sacrificial cult. The references in the following verse in Deut. 23:18 to harlot and dog, the latter of which may point to a male prostitute, also lead one to favor this interpretation, cf. Horner, *Jonathan Loved David*, pp. 59–70. The purpose of the prostitute would be to symbolize the power of the fertility god. The reformers who stand behind the Deuteronomic legislation fought for the explusion of such figures from Israelite religion, but we find references to their existence in the cult from the tenth century until the late seventh, when the Deuteronomists with the support of Josiah perhaps finally won. Cf. 1 Kings 14:24, 15:12, 22:46; 2 Kings 23:7. The same word appears also in Job 36:14 but the meaning is unclear. It is interesting to note that in the Chronicles, a later retelling of the events in Kings, the references to the male prostitute have all been eliminated.

7. *E.g.*, Horner, *Jonathan Loved David*, pp. 65f; McNeill, *Church and the Homosexual*, p. 57.

8. So also John Boswell, *Christianity, Social Tolerance, and Homosexuality*, p. 99; UPC, *The Church and Homosexuality* (New York: Office of the General Assembly, 1978), pp. 18f; Bailey, *Homosexuality and the Western Christian Tradition* (New York and London: Longmans, Green & Co., 1955), pp. 52f.; J. Gray, *I & II Kings*, (Philadelphia: Westminster Press, 1963), p. 311; and G. von Rad, *Deuteronomy*, (Philadelphia: Westminster Press, 1966), pp. 147f, skirt the issue.

9. Anymore than the prohibition of the female prostitute is a general indictment of heterosexuality.

fourth centuries B.C.E. does an explicit law emerge which deals with male homosexuality in general (Lev. 18:22; 20:13).[10] The prohibition in Lev. 18:22 is terse: "With a male you shall not lie (*shakav*) the lyings of a woman; it is an abomination" (au. trans.). The awkwardness of the sentence is caused by the fact that there is no technical term for homosexuality in Hebrew. Nevertheless the meaning is clear. *Shakav* is frequently used to denote sexual intercourse; thus the sentence is a general prohibition of male homosexuality.[11]

Two things must be noted. The first is that female homosexuality is not prohibited. The second is the wording of the verse. This is important to observe since a constitution will frequently determine the language of subseq ent interpretations and analyses. There is more to note than the lack of a technical term and the use of a euphemism (*shakav*) for intercourse. What is crucial is that the general word for "male" is used, without any qualification of age. This lack of qualification will determine the *language* of all future Jewish discussions, no matter what forms of homosexuality are being attacked. As we shall see, Paul is no exception to this rule.

Leviticus 20 gives the variou. penalties to be imposed on the practices scored in chapter 18. The penalty for male homosexuality is death, although no specific form of execution is assigned. "If a man lies with a male as with a woman, both of them have committed an abomination; they shall be put to death, their blood is upon them" (v. 13). Male homosexuality is but one of several crimes listed as punishable by death in this chapter; that is, it is not singled out as a uniquely heinous sin. Otherwise, the same

10. The commonly accepted theory is that the present form of the Pentateuch, with the inclusion of all of the legal material ascribed to Moses, stems from the work of the priests in the postexilic period. There is no reasonable doubt that the Holiness Code (Leviticus 17—26), a set of legal traditions in which the law in question is found, existed prior to its incorporation in the Priestly laws, but it is impossible to know whether it enjoyed wide acceptance or acted as an effective part of Israelite law before that time.

11. Leviticus 18 has a clear literary structure. At beginning and end are warnings against practices of the Egyptians and Canaanites. In between are listings, presumably, of what these abhorred practices were, with prohibitions against doing them. It has been suggested that these prohibitions were thus originally linked with pagan, perhaps even pagan cultic activities; even if that should be the case, in its present form the text remains a general indictment.

comments made about Lev. 18:22 are applicable here. No mention is made about female homosexuality; the terms are the general ones for man and male; and intercourse is pointed to euphemistically.

These two verses are the only legal traditions about homosexuality in the Hebrew Bible. Furthermore, no other biblical passage refers to this prohibition, nor is there any story showing the law being applied in a concrete situation. All that can be said is that late in Israelite history a single law appears (although it may have had an earlier existence) prohibiting male homosexuality. No rationale is given for its appearance as an "abomination." One might conjecture that originally it was linked to pagan religious culture or with the thwarting of the intended use of semen for purposes of procreation, but it is probably best not to speculate.[12]

2. *Stories.* There are two ancient stories which have always seemed to suggest a hostile biblical attitude toward homosexuality. The most famous is, of course, the story of Sodom and Gomorrah (Genesis 19). Angels have come to destroy the cities because of their grave sinfulness, although the sin is not specified in Gen. 18:20, where the intended destruction is announced. When Lot offers hospitality to the two "men," the evil males of Sodom encompass the house to try to force Lot to send the guests out: "Bring them out to us, that we may know them" (19:5). Lot tries to divert their attention to his two daughters, virgins "who have not known man" (19:8). The evil men persist, however, in wanting the male guests, hence sealing the doom of Sodom. Since the Hebrew verb, "to know," can be used in the sense "to have sexual intercourse with," and since the use of that word with regard to Lot's daughters demands a sexual meaning, it has traditionally been thought that the men of Sodom intend to violate the bodies of the male guests. While this interpretation has recently been called into question, it seems to me difficult to deny the sexual intent of the Sodomites. I still believe the traditional interpretation to be correct.[13]

12. Cf. the discussion in Horner, *Jonathan Loved David*, pp. 71–85.
13. The argument against a homosexual interpretation includes the following claims. (1) Elsewhere the verb, "to know," when used to point to sexual intercourse, occurs only in heterosexual contexts. (2) In the Sodom story the men simply want to identify just who the strangers are who have come into their city and

Any claim, however, that the story is a blanket condemnation of homosexuality in general is unjustified. The attempt on the bodies of the guests is but an example of the general evil, which has already caught God's attention. It is, furthermore, an attempt at *rape*.[14] The most that can be said is that the story judges homosexual rape to be evil and worthy of condemnation.

Scholars have noted that virtually none of the other references to this story in the Hebrew Bible (unless it is that of the Levite and his concubine) explicitly interpret the sin as sexual.[15] The story functions in these later references generally as a symbol of human wickedness and/or God's punishment.[16] Later biblical authors thus had no apparent interest in the homosexual dimension of this story.

The long narrative in Judges 19 about the Levite and his concubine is in some respects closely related to that in Genesis 19 and, according to some scholars, is dependent on it.[17] After telling about the estrangement and reconciliation of the pair, the story describes the journey home of the two. On the way they spend the

---

why they are there (to know in that sense). (3) The sin is their inhospitality toward the strangers. (4) In subsequent references to the story of Sodom in the Bible (including the New Testament) there is rarely if ever any indication it was seen as intended homosexual rape. Such views are held by Bailey, *Homosexuality and the Western Christian Tradition*, pp. 1–28; McNeill, *Church and the Homosexual*, pp. 42–50; Boswell, *Christianity, Social Tolerance, and Homosexuality*, pp. 92–97. For a careful inspection of the arguments cf. A. M. J. M. Herman van de Spijker, *Die gleichgeschlectliche Zuneigung* (Olten: Walter Verlag, 1968), pp. 67–74. He concludes against Bailey that the Sodomites do have homosexual intentions.

14. It is true that the Hebrew terms used for rape do not appear in the account. If, however, the story has sexual dimensions at all, the intended act can only be seen as rape—and gang rape at that! So also Horner, *Jonathan Loved David*, p. 50; UPC, *Church and Homosexuality*, p. 17; van de Spijker, *Die gleichgeschlectliche Zuneigung*, pp. 73f.

15. E.g., Boswell: "Sodom is used as a symbol of evil in dozens of places, but not in a single instance is the sin of the Sodomites specified as homosexuality" (*Christianity, Social Tolerance, and Homosexuality*, p. 94).

16. Cf. Amos 4:11; Isa. 1:9–10; 13:19; Jer. 49:18; Lam. 4:6; Ezek. 16:46, 48–49, 53, 55–56; Zeph. 2:9; Deut. 29:22; 32:32. The only possible exception is Ezek. 16:49–50. "Behold, this was the guilt of your sister Sodom: she and her daughters had pride, surfeit of food, and prosperous ease, but did not aid the poor and needy. They were haughty, and did abominable things before me." The word "abominable" is the same as that found in the Leviticus prohibition and could possibly refer to homosexuality, although the word is very general and should not be pressed.

17. E.g., G. F. Moore, *Judges* (New York: Charles Scribner's Sons, 1900), p. 417; H. W. Hertzberg, *Die Bücher Josua, Richter, Ruth* (Göttingen: Vandenhoeck & Ruprecht, 1959), p. 252.

night at Gibeah, which they think is safe because it is inhabited by Israelites. Received into the home of an old man, the same scene occurs as narrated in Genesis 19, except that now it is Israelites who are the evildoers! The men of the city call out to the host: "Bring out the man who came into your house, that we may know him" (v. 22). Women—the host's virgin daughter and the Levite's concubine—are then offered as a substitute, in language reminiscent of Gen. 19:8. The concubine is, in fact, thrown out to the men. They violate her all night until she is dead. Here the verb "to know" almost surely refers to a sexual desire for homosexual rape. If this story is in fact dependent on that about Sodom, it provides us with the earliest interpretation of Genesis 19, in which, contrary to later references, the homosexual dimension of the story of Sodom is accepted.

Summary. Some researchers have believed there are further stories and materials in the Hebrew Bible which refer to homosexuality.[18] Still others have dealt with theological assertions and presuppositions in the Bible which would influence and determine biblical attitudes.[19] I have confined discussion to those few passages which postbiblical Jews might read, or did read, as referring to homosexuality. It is necessary now to analyze these postbiblical discussions to realize the potential horizons of early Jewish Christian interpretations of the biblical constitution.

POSTBIBLICAL PALESTINIAN JEWISH TRADITIONS

1. *The Targums.* As already suggested, Palestinian Jews by the time of the New Testament heard the biblical message in Aramaic. The texts we now possess of the Targums may have originated as oral translations given during the synagogue services and later collected together. Of course it is impossible to know whether the Targums Jews of the first century *heard* in the syna-

18. E.g., David and Jonathan, Ruth and Naomi. Cf. Horner, *Jonathan Loved David*, pp. 26–46.

19. E.g., the creation narratives, cf. McNeill, *Church and the Homosexual*, pp. 60–66; creation and fall, cf. H. Thielicke, *The Ethics of Sex* (New York: Harper & Row, 1964), pp. 281–87.

gogues are accurately reflected in the extant *documents* we now possess, but these at least will give us some indication of the kinds of interpretations the Jewish community was giving its constitution.[20]

The legal materials. The Palestinian Targums translate the laws in Leviticus literally with, if anything, a less euphemistic verb.[21] Their treatment of Deut. 23:18, however, causes surprise. Ignoring the cultic dimension of the biblical text, Neofiti translates: "Let there be no woman from the daughters of Israel who is a prostitute, nor a male prostitute from the sons of Israel."[22] The prohibition is taken to refer to *secular* male as well as female prostitution, and that must mean male homosexual prostitution. As we shall see below rabbinic discussions also take the verse in Deuteronomy to refer to male homosexual activities.

Does this mean that in the time of Paul male prostitution had invaded Palestinian Jewish culture? No sure answer can be given, but if translations bend the text to make it speak to issues relevant

20. There are two distinct targumic traditions reflected in the manuscripts. One is represented by so-called Pseudo-Jonathan and the recently published Neofiti 1 and is often felt to be the earlier tradition, reflecting the Aramaic dialect and theological traditions of Jewish Palestine. The second is named Targum Onkelos and is often claimed to represent a later, Babylonian Jewish tradition. Scholars are still disputing the matter, however, and while I will use the traditional designations, Palestinian and Babylonian, in my discussion, the reader should know that no clear consensus has yet been reached. For a brief discussion of the issues, cf. S. Lund and J. Foster, *Variant Versions of Targumic Traditions within Codex Neofiti 1* (Missoula, Mont.: Scholars Press, 1977), p. 113. I have relied on the following printed versions of the mss.: *Targum Jonathan ben Uziel*, edited by D. Rieder (Jerusalem, 1974); *Neofiti 1*, 6 vols, edited by A. Diez Macho (Madrid: Consejo Superior de Investigaciones Científices 1968–80); *The Pentateuch according to Targum Onkelos*, A. Sperber (Leiden: E. J. Brill, 1959).

21. Both Neofiti and Pseudo-Jonathan use *shamash*, a word that frequently means "to have intercourse with." Pseudo-Jonathan, furthermore, denotes in 20:13 the means of execution as stoning, a tradition found also in *San* 7.4.

22. Pseudo-Jonathan uses a more general phrase with regard to the male. It *could* point to heterosexual fornication rather than prostitution. I take Neofiti to interpret the meaning of Pseudo-Jonathan. Targum Onkelos moves even further afield from the original meaning of the verse in Deuteronomy. "Let no Israelite woman belong to a male slave, and let no male Israelite marry a female slave." The point is that Targums can easily move away from literal meanings when other considerations are at stake. On the other hand the Hebrew word for "sacral prostitute" appears in Gen. 38:21–22 in a context of apparently secular prostitution. A reader of that passage would naturally think *qedeshah* meant secular prostitution, and Neofiti so translates it. It is also instructive to see that Targum Jonathan has eliminated any reference to male prostitutes in the relevant passages in Kings (cf. note 6 above).

to the translators, the possibility must at least be taken seriously. At the least the text is a prohibition against assuming a role similar to that we have identified as the effeminate call-boy.

The stories in the Bible. The Palestinian Targums translate the story of Sodom and Gomorrah faithfully. At the places where the Hebrew word "to know" is used in the Hebrew, Neofiti chooses the verb, *hacham*, literally "to be wise," which has as a metaphorical meaning, "to have sexual intercourse." That is, the Aramaic has the same ambiguity as the Hebrew.[23] Pseudo-Jonathan, however, is more explicit. This text uses at the passages in question the same verb for sexual intercourse that both it and Neofiti use in the prohibitions in Lev. 18:22 and 20:13. Thus, at least for Pseudo-Jonathan, there is no question but that it understands the intended act to be homosexual rape. Pseudo-Jonathan is not, however, consistent. In the story in Judges the Aramaic verb "to know" is used.

2. *Early Rabbinic Legal Discussions.* Since male homosexuality is prohibited in the Bible, it is hardly surprising that early rabbinic legal discussions include the topic. These discussions are not, however, extensive; in fact they rarely occur. The reader must keep also in mind an unusual feature of many rabbinic texts. Legal debates normally assume the reality of the crime and the actuality of a court system in which punishment can be carried out. In rabbinic law, however, discussions may take place about nonexistent realities as if they existed (e.g., Temple rites) and for which, apparently, punitive measures were no longer possible. Thus it is precarious in such instances to take the discussions too literally. They may say little or nothing about actual practices or effective court or penal controls over people who violate the statutes set up by the rabbis. This is particularly true about issues which theoretically involve the death penalty.[24] We can, however, at least see what these early lawyers thought the biblical texts prohibited and the attitudes they held toward homosexual practices.

In the primary law code of this period (*The Mishnah*) male ho-

23. This is Neofiti's usual word to translate the Hebrew "to know" when it has a sexual meaning. Cf. Gen. 4:1, 17, 25; 24:16; 38:26.

24. By the time the rabbinic laws were being codified, it is highly unlikely any Jewish court had the power of execution.

mosexuality is included among the crimes punishable with death by stoning (the Bible did not specify the means of execution).[25] In the Babylonian Talmud's commentary on this mishnah, an exegetical rationale for this penalty is given, with the verses in Leviticus providing a basis for the argument.[26] A fairly detailed discussion of the interpretation of the laws takes place, with a number of contributions made by rabbis from the early period. The arguments are intricate and I can only give the basic conclusions. One presupposition they hold in common with Greco-Roman discussion: the same distinction is made between the active and the passive partner, although it is acknowledged that the same person could be both active and passive. This distinction must have been derived from the cultural context rather than the biblical text, although, as rabbis are wont to do, the distinction is tied to the text.

In this talmudic passage, the rabbis see an age distinction in the verse that describes the penalty for homosexual activity (Lev. 20:13). The active partner is culpable only if he is an adult (since the passage begins: "If a man"); the passive partner is culpable at whatever age (since the verse continues: "lies with a male"). This creates a problem for them, since they interpret the prohibition in Lev. 18:22 to pertain only to a active partner (since the wording, "you shall not lie," they take to be directed against the active role). The dilemma is that we have a prohibition seemingly only against the active partner, but a penalty directed against both active and passive. According to rabbinic sensibilities, there can be no penalty without a prohibition.

The scholars find a way out through Deut. 23:18.[27] It has already been indicated that the Palestinian Targums take the male prostitute here to be a secular prostitute. The rabbis, assuming that such a prostitute would take the passive role, find in the Deu-

25. *San.* 7.4.
26. *San.* 54a–b. The involved discussion is linked to both early and later rabbinical authorities. In the discussion that follows I give the judgments only of the early figures. Cf. also T*San.* 10.2; p*San.* 7, 24d–25a; *Sifra, Qedoshim, perek* 9, par. 14.
27. It is true that the verse in Deuteronomy is somewhat artificially drawn into this discussion by word association, using Lev. 18:22, 1 Kings 14:24, and Deut. 23:18 (the rule of *gezerah shavah*). I am confident, however, that the association of meaning was prior to the rabbinic hermeneutic.

teronomic verse the prohibition against the passive partner they need. Thus once again in postbiblical discussion, Deut. 23:18 is drawn into debate about secular homosexual activity, whatever the original meaning of the verse may have been. One cannot be sure that the rabbis have in mind something similer to the call-boy that we have seen derided in the Greco-Roman debates; at the least, they clearly identify the male prostitute with the passive role in a homosexual relationship.

Does this discussion imply that the rabbis thought homosexuality, or pederasty, existed within Judaism of their day? That the rabbis believed Jewish males *might* be tempted is indicated in another set of traditions which belong to the category of "putting a fence around the Torah," that is, of eliminating conditions which might lead to a violation of the law. One law states: "An unmarried man may not be a teacher of children, nor may a woman be a teacher of children. R. Eliezer says: Even a man that has no wife [meaning obscure, perhaps, no wife presently living with him] may not be a teacher of children. R. Judah says: "An unmarried man may not herd cattle, nor may two unmarried men sleep under the same cloak. But the Sages permit it."[28] Bringing a man who has no regular outlet for his sexual energies into a classroom situation (in which the students would be largely, if not entirely, male) throws him into the danger of temptation. The same temptation lurks when two single men sleep close to one another. Hence, in order to remove temptations, these situations are prohibited. This last prohibition is, however, overruled by "the Sages" (usually taken as pointing to the majority view). That is, the Sages do not think Israelite male temptation a real possibility. Elsewhere the rule is worded slightly differently. "A single man shall not be a shepherd nor shall two single men sleep under the same cloak." But just as above, the need for such a fence is rejected by a rejoinder in the next sentence: "Israel is not suspected [of males who would be tempted to engage in homosexuality or bestiality]."[29]

---

28. *Kid.* 4.13f. I use the translation by Herbert Danby, *The Mishnah* (London: Oxford Univ. Press, 1933), p. 329. The prohibition against the single male teacher certainly implies a pederastic model.

29. T*Kid.* 5.10; cf. also *Kid.* 82a.

Since female homosexuality is never mentioned in the Bible, it is not surprising that the legal discussions virtually ignore it. To my knowledge only one early mention of it occurs in a legal context. Here the issue concerns what Israelite woman is qualified to marry a priest. According to the Bible (Lev. 21:7, 13–14) she must be a virgin. Premarital intercourse with a man obviously disqualifies the woman from such a marriage. What, however, about a woman's sexual relationships with another woman? Does this count as losing virginity? The famous and powerful houses of Hillel and Shammai disputed the matter. "Two women who have sex with each other: the house of Shammai disqualifies, but the house of Hillel permits [the women to marry a priest]."[30] Obviously, from a legal perspective, female homosexuality was of little interest and, at least by the Hillelites, not taken with much seriousness.

3. *Reflection upon the Stories in the Bible.* Not many traditions about Sodom can be traced to early rabbinic times. Such as do exist follow the tendency in the Bible to define the sin of the Sodomites as something other than homosexual lust. A quite early judgment by Ben Sirach suggests its sin was pride.[31] In other passages the Sodomites, among other groups, are said to have no share in the world to come because of their evil, but what that evil was thought to consist of is not mentioned.[32]

A lively and playful interpretation of the sins of the Sodomites appears in a text which in its final form is later than our period, but which includes several contributions from early rabbis.[33] These early rabbis picture the Sodomites as totally perverse, standing all sorts of justice on its head. Numerous examples are given (including a version of Procrustes' bed!). Among the vices listed are sexual sins as well as those of greediness and pride. *Never*, however, is there any hint of homosexual lust or activity. The sexual sins are all heterosexual.[34] The Palestinian Targum's

---

30. p*Git.* 49*c*, 70.
31. *Sirach* 16:8. For the Hebrew, cf. S. Schechter and C. Taylor, *The Wisdom of Ben Sira* (Cambridge: Cambridge Univ. Press, 1899).
32. E.g., *San.* 10.3.
33. *San.* 109*a–b*.
34. For other "economic" interpretations of Sodom's sin, cf. *B.B.* 12*b*, 59*a*, 168*a*; *Erub.* 49*a*; *Ket.* 103*a*.

clear statement of the sin as sexual does not, perhaps surprisingly, seem to have informed rabbinic midrash of this time.

It is possible that one rabbi of our period does give a sexual interpretation to the story.[35] Accredited to him in one source is a saying in which the same explicit verb for sexual intercourse that appeared in Pseudo-Jonathan's translation of Genesis 19 and Lev. 18:22; 20:13 is used to indicate the sin of the Sodomites. But this is a rare voice. For rabbis of this period, Sodom symbolized evil in general, pride and economic violence most particularly, and only in one possible instance homosexual lust.

4. *Homosexuality as a Gentile Vice.* For the rabbis, at least, homosexuality is certainly a Gentile, not a Jewish, sin. We have already noted that the reply to the opinion that two Jewish males should not sleep under the same cloak is that "Israel is not suspected" of such activities. In an interpretation of Lev. 18:3, where Moses warns the Israelites not to imitate the vices of Egypt and Canaan, one vice attributed to the pagans is both male and female homosexual marriage.[36]

Occasionally this attitude reaches into legal or quasi-legal discussions. One tradition warns against sending a Jewish youth to a Gentile to study, learn a trade, or even to be alone with—obviously for fear the youth will be used for pederastic purposes.[37] Here is one of the occasional allusions in this literature to the pederastic model. On one occasion during the period we are studying, the Shammaites (usually seen to be in the minority) outnumbered the Hillelites in the academy and voted eighteen decrees against the prevailing Hillelite opinions.[38] No one seems to have remembered exactly what these decrees were. Not surprisingly there was later speculation. According to a later rabbi, one

---

35. Bar Kappara in *Lev.R.* 23.9. The problem is that elsewhere (*Gen. R.* 26.5, 50.5) the saying is attributed to a later rabbi (Padiah). The verb is, of course, *shamash.*

36. *Sifra* Lev. 18:3, *Ahare Moth, perek* 9, par. 8. Cf. also *perek* 13, par. 8. Other people in the biblical stories, when it is clear they are non-Israelites, were burdened with the vices of homosexuality—the generation of the flood (who wrote marriage songs for males and beasts!), Potiphar, Nebuchadnezzar, the "watchers" of Genesis 6, and perhaps Queen Vashti. Traditions in *Gen. R.* 26.5; *Lev. R.* 23.9; *Est. R.* III. 2; *Sot.* 13*b*; *Sab.* 149*b*.

37. TA.Z. 10.2.

38. *Sab.* 1.4.

was designed to protect Jewish youths from Gentile homosexual lust. All Gentile youths were declared by the Shammaites to be legally ill with gonorrhea so that Jewish youths could not be tempted to associate with them for homosexual purposes (although this shows the temptation was feared to be a real possibility).[39] One would have to be skeptical about the historicity of this speculation; it may only show the measures one later rabbi would like to have seen taken. Here is another "fence around the Torah."

All is summed up in one passage, granted, from a later source, in which Jacob and Esau are being contrasted. Esau here stands for Rome and its culture. A rabbi complains that Esau is promiscuous. Israel cries out for relief from God against this oppressor. "Must we not only serve other nations but this one as well, with whom one has intercourse like a woman?"[40]

5. *Jewish Homosexuality?* The question has to be raised about evidence for homosexual activity among the Jews themselves of this period, however much "Israel is not suspected." Most of the legal materials discussed above could be seen as directed toward Jews, since Jewish courts had no jurisdiction over Gentiles. The various rules which "put a fence around the Torah" show especially a sensitivity to the possibility of such activity among Jews. Whatever the realities might be that lie behind these materials, some legislators clearly wished to take no chances.[41]

All of this, however, floats in the air. Nothing can be proved from them and *without concrete stories*, such as we could make such use of in the Greco-Roman materials, no real conclusions about the actual existence of Jewish homosexuality can be drawn. The argument from silence is dangerous here (i.e., since there are no stories, there was no homosexuality) because such relationships would have had to be closeted. To the best of my knowledge, there is only *one* story in the literature about an event contempo-

---

39. *Sab.* 17b.
40. *Gen. R.* 63.10.
41. In *San.* 54a one discussion about homosexuality directs it against Gentiles, but a rabbi there admits this is a euphemism for Israel. That is, in his view homosexuality is a reality to be legislated against within the Jewish community. For other texts which might or clearly do suggest male homosexuality an actuality within Judaism (most of these are later) cf. *Suk.* 29a; *San.* 82a; p*Ber.* 9, 13a, 50.

rary to the rabbis themselves, and this is reported of a rabbi from the later period. Judah ben Pazzi once climbed to the upper story of a *beth midrash* (the Jewish schoolhouse) and discovered two males having intercourse with one another. "They said to him, 'rabbi, take note that you are one and we are two.'"[42] The point of the retort is that two witnesses who agree are necessary in a Jewish court to prove wrongdoing. The men could falsify their witness and the rabbi's single affirmation could not overrule theirs, no matter how false theirs was. The point for us, however, is that the rabbi discovered two males, doubtlessly Jewish and knowledgeable about the legal niceties, having homosexual intercourse. To generalize from this one account is precarious. There may well have been some male homosexuality among Jews; but if so it did not trouble seriously the rabbinic conscience.

6. *Rabbinic Terminology for Male Homosexuality.* As already shown, there was no Hebrew—or, for that matter, Aramaic—word for homosexuality. When the Bible raises the issue, as we have seen, it points to it by the awkward phrase, "With a male you shall not lie the lyings of a woman" (au. trans.) (Lev. 18:22), or, "A man who lies with a male the lyings of a woman" (au. trans.) (Lev. 20:13). Rabbinic scholars picked up part of that phrase, "lies with a male," made it virtually into a noun, and gave it nearly the status of a technical term. The term that thus emerged and that is used frequently in this literature is *mishkav zakur* (lying of a male) or *mishkav bzakur* (lying with a male).[43] Later I will argue that this Hebrew expression lies behind the rare Greek word, *arsenokoitēs* (lit. lying of, with a male) in 1 Cor. 6:9.

CONCLUSIONS

Let me now try to draw together the conclusions proper to this diverse material, which is partly severely legal and logical, partly imaginative and fanciful.

1. The Hebrew Bible provides the basis for the majority of the discussions. It is the raw material, both with regard to content and

42. p*San.* 6, 23*c*, 4.
43. Cf. e.g., *Sifra, Qedoshim, perek* 9, par. 14; *Sifra, Ahare Moth, perek* 13, par. 8; *Sab.* 17*b*; *Suk.* 29*a*; *San.* 82*a*; p*Ber.* 9, 13*c*, 50.

to language, out of which Palestinian Jews fashioned their own traditions about homosexuality. Thus the *language* of the Bible, the manner of expressing the content, guides and controls the language of the rabbis. The terms are resolutely male with male, never adult with youth, even when the rabbis are discussing age differential. Lev. 20:13 probably lies behind the semitechnical term the rabbis coined for male homosexuality.

2. Distinction between the active and the passive partner is the one feature in which commonality between Jewish and Greco-Roman discussions is evident. No more than among Greeks and Romans was there awareness of adult-adult mutual relationships.

3. Jewish culture in its official form was entirely opposed to male homosexuality and, presumably, to female as well.

4. The discussion is conducted *as if* both male and female homosexuality were possible realities within the Jewish community, although it is mostly Gentiles who are specifically accused. What forms such Jewish homosexuality may have taken, if it existed, cannot be learned from the texts.

5. The discussion is entirely directed toward the sexual act and its culpability. Nothing is ever said about any other possible dimension of the relationship. Indeed, from this discussion alone, one would assume a homosexual encounter to be only for purposes of sexual gratification, as if other qualities of a possible friendship either were irrelevant, unimportant, or perhaps nonexistent. Greco-Roman culture was more receptive to such personal values and more compassionate in understanding the human dynamic of homosexuality than was the Jewish, at least to judge from the textual evidence. This is also true of Hellenistic Jewish attitudes, which, if anything, were more homophobic than Palestinian.

These positions and attitudes of Palestinian Judaism (along with those of Hellenistic Judaism) were influential on New Testament views and, in part, on its language. I move to a conclusion which can be tentatively formulated in this way: The homosexuality the New Testament opposes is the pederasty of the Greco-Roman culture; the attitudes toward pederasty and, in part, the language used to oppose it are informed by the Jewish background.

6
Hellenistic Judaism:
Pederasty Vilified

With the culture of Hellenistic Judaism we reach the milieu which is closest to that of the New Testament churches. In fact it might even be possible to say that the New Testament writings are one manifestation of that culture. Hellenistic Jews seem to have *written* the majority of the New Testament documents. And while Palestinian Jewish concerns are certainly present in places, particularly in the Gospels, the majority of *readers* must have been rooted in the culture of Hellenism, either Jewish or pagan. Paul is a product of the crossfertilization of Palestinian with Hellenistic Jewish cultures. Long before Paul, however, the process of acculturation between Judaism and Hellenism had begun in the Diaspora. Hellenistic Judaism is thus itself already a result of the interweaving of two cultures. For this reason it is particularly important to pay attention both to the language and content of these expressions, if one wishes to understand the message of the New Testament.

THE SEPTUAGINT (LXX)

Just as it was necessary to begin study of postbiblical Palestinian Judaism with the translation of the Bible into Aramaic, so here one must take the same beginning point: the translation of the Bible into Greek, called the Septuagint (LXX). This is our earliest evidence for Hellenistic Judaism.

1. *Laws.* Lev. 18:22, 20:13. The Hebrew is translated faithfully and it is important to see the words the translator chose. "With a male [*arsen*] you shall not lie the intercourse [*koitē*: lit. "bed"] of a

85

woman" (18:22). "And whoever lies with a male [*arsen*] the intercourse [*koitē*] of a woman, both have done an abomination; they shall be put to death, they are guilty" (20:13). What is instructive to note is the juxtaposition of the two words *arsen* and *koitē*; these are the two roots of the compound noun that appears in 1 Cor. 6:9, *arsenokoitēs*. In the previous chapter I noted that the rabbis, using the comparable words from Leviticus, coined a phrase for male homosexuality which reached almost semitechnical status, *mishkav zekor* (lying with a male). *Arsenokoitēs* is an almost exact Greek parallel to the Hebrew and is equally derived from Leviticus. More than ever the evidence suggests that *arsenokoitēs* is a Hellenistic Jewish coinage, perhaps influenced by awareness of rabbinic terminology.

Deut. 23:17–18. Although this passage in the Hebrew original was probably a reference to cultic heterosexual prostitution, we have seen how it was drawn by postbiblical Palestinian Jewish traditions into the issue of secular male homosexuality. This occurred (*a*) in the Palestinian Targum's reworking of the verse into a general prohibition against Israelite male and female prostitution and (*b*) in the rabbinic legal materials where it is taken to be a prohibition against the passive partner in homosexual activity. Thus whatever the parameters of the verse in the original context, the Palestinian Jew interpreted it in relation to homosexuality.

The Septuagint draws the passage in the same direction, although in a curiously ambiguous way. Instead of a single statement, two appear here, both in exact parallelism with each other. "There shall not be a female prostitute among the daughters of Israel, nor shall a male prostitute [himself] among the sons of Israel. There shall not be a *telesphoros* among the daughters of Israel, nor shall there be a *teliskomenos* among the sons of Israel" (LXX, v. 18). The meaning of the terms left untranslated is uncertain, except that they both have to do with Greek religious cultic terminology. Thus, apparently, the second statement prohibits any Israelite from participating in foreign cults (this is how Philo will understand the passage). What is remarkable here is that we seem to have two different translations of the Hebrew original standing in parallelism, as if the translators, instead of

making a decision about the by-then problematic Hebrew meaning, accepted two different traditions and included both of them.
However that may be, the Septuagint contains here a prohibition
against secular male homosexual prostitution, *exactly as does the
Palestinian Targum.*[1]

2. *Stories.* Sodom, and the Levite and his concubine. The relevant passages are translated faithfully to the Hebrew. The usual
Greek word "to know" (*ginōskō*) can also, just as the Hebrew
equivalent, have the meaning "to have sexual intercourse with."
In the instances where the Hebrew verb "to know" is used in the
Bible for sexual intercourse, the Septuagint translators use
ginōskō. This is true in Gen. 19:8 with reference to Lot's daughters, and in both relevant instances in the story of the Levite and
his concubine. It is not the case, however, with Gen. 19:5. Here
the translators chose *sunginomai*, the literal meaning of which is to
"associate," "keep company with." It can also have, however, the
meaning "to have sexual intercourse with," both for homosexual
as well as heterosexual acts.[2] Since *sunginomai* has the same ambiguity of meaning as *ginōskō*, we can learn nothing from the translation which reveals the understanding the translators had of the
intended act of the Sodomites.

1. It is possible to argue against this conclusion on the basis of linguistic evidence. The Greek verb in the phrase "nor shall a male prostitute [himself]" is the
participle, *porneuōn*. In normal Greek usage, this verb primarily refers to the act of
prostituting a person, or self. In the LXX and New Testament, it can be argued
that the verb sometimes has a more general meaning, including all kinds of illegal
sexual activity. Thus this half of the sentence *could* refer to a man who used the
services of the female prostitute attacked in the previous clause. Such a reading,
however, seems to me unlikely. In the other appearances of this verb in the Septuagint, virtually all of them do refer either to literal prostitution or to the metaphorical sense of people prostituting themselves in following after other gods. The
RSV, for example, normally gives as the translation, "to play the harlot." It is to be
granted that in a few instances, the difference between prostitution and more general fornication in the metaphorical occurrences is slight. In the passages where
the usage is literal, however, actual prostitution is the subject. Cf. Hos. 3:3; 4:14;
Amos 7:17. Only in Hos. 4:18 in all of the nineteen appearances in the Septuagint
is there a participial use, and that is not really parallel to Deut. 23:17. It may thus
be that the participle in Deuteronomy is really used as a noun, although, it is true,
the translator could have used the noun (*pornos*) if that is what he had in mind. Inspection of the related verb, *exporneuein*, leads to the same conclusions.

2. For the use of the verb in a pederastic context (with *pais*), cf. *Inscriptiones
Graecae*, ed. F. H. de Gaertringen, Editio Minor, Vol. IV, Fasc. 1 (Berlin: Walter
de Gruyter, 1929), Inscription II, 121, lines 104f.

HELLENISTIC JEWISH DISCUSSIONS

1. *Laws.* We do not have access to the same wealth of legal tradition in Hellenistic Judaism that is extant in rabbinic literature. Yet Philo, for all his interest in allegorization, does on occasion provide us with an interpretation of the text from a literal point of view, that is, what *he* thinks the laws mean.

Lev. 18:22; 20:13. When Philo discusses these laws he introduces the topic with the following sentence. "Much graver than the above [marriages with barren women] is another evil, which has ramped its way into the cities, namely pederasty."[3] The entire discussion which follows centers on pederasty and what Philo considers disgraceful about it. *Thus it is clear that when Philo reads the general laws in his Bible against male homosexuality he is thinking entirely about the cultural manifestation in his own environment.*

He distinguishes between the active and the passive partner. His greatest scorn is poured out on the effeminate male, the callboy, attacking the coiffuring of hair, the use of cosmetics and perfume, the general effort to turn his male nature into the female. In fact he labels the effeminate male *androgynos* (lit. male-female), a term of reproach which has rarely occurred in the Greco-Roman texts we have inspected in previous chapters.[4] These androgynous creatures have infiltrated into the ranks of the Greek cults where they are highly honored, Philo moans, and some of them have gone so far as to accept castration. "These persons are rightly judged worthy of death by those who obey the Law." This statement is directed against the *androgynos*, but Philo does not

---

3. *Special Laws* III. 37. For the entire discussion cf. 37–42. The passages here are cited from the translation of F. H. Colson, *Philo*, VII, LCL (Cambridge, Mass.: Harvard Univ. Press, 1958).

4. The word does appear in Aristophanes' speech in Plato's *Symposium*, where he uses it neutrally to refer to the original union of the male/female creature, although he acknowledges the term is actually one of reproach (189E). Aeschines implies that his enemy Demosthenes is *androgynos* in *On the Embassy* 127—again obviously a derogatory comment. The word even appears twice in the LXX Proverbs (18:8; 19:15) as a term of reproach (there is little relation between the Greek and Hebrew in these verses). In early rabbinic law the *androgynos* is a legal category, referring to a person who in some undefined way exhibits characteristics of both sexes. The term, however, as far as I can tell is not used here derogatorily. Cf. *Bik.* ch. 4.

forget those who use them. "And the lover (*paiderastēs*) of such may be assured that he is subject to the same penalty." It is crucial to note that when he *reads* the general law against homosexuality, he is *thinking* about male prostitution and those who buy the service of such youths.

In this passage the reasons Philo gives for his hostility to pederasty are twofold. First, both the active and the passive partner are acting against nature (*para phusin*). The *androgynos* is a counterfeit coin, while the pederast pursues an unnatural pleasure. Second, the greatest sin, however, and Philo is emphatic about it, is the channeling of semen away from its divinely intended purpose—procreation. The pederast "does his best to render cities desolate and uninhabited by destroying the means of procreation." Philo attacks this misuse wherever he finds it. In fact the passage on pederasty follows immediately after an assault on what for Philo is a serious crime, even though it is not so stated in the Bible: males who mate with barren women. His language is strong. "Those persons who make an art of quenching the life of the seed as it drops, stand confessed as the enemies of nature."[5]

Deut. 23:1. Philo introduces a verse into the discussion which has so far not figured. "He whose testicles are crushed or whose male member is cut off shall not enter the assembly of the Lord." This verse, which seems to have been an attempt to exclude people considered unclean (i.e., not whole) from polluting the purity of the sacred community, cannot have had anything directly to do with homosexuality. Philo, however, takes it to refer to the effeminate male, again called *androgynos*, who falsifies his true nature and attempts to turn himself into a woman. He seems to be taking castration figuratively here, although he may be thinking also of those who are literally castrated for such purposes.[6] An especially

---

5. Philo, *Special Laws* III. 36. In another treatise (*Hypothetica* 7.1) Philo mentions pederasty as a crime punishable by death, again indicating that he is thinking about pederasty when he reads the general prohibition in Lev. 20:13. Josephus also once mentions the laws in Leviticus against homosexuality, but he retains the general terms found in the Bible ("male with male"), cf. Jos. *Against Apion* II. 199–200.

6. Philo, *Special Laws* I. 325.

ardent opponent of this form of pederasty, Philo looks for every opportunity to attack it.

Deut. 23:17–18. Philo evidences knowledge of both statements in the Greek version of 23:17, but none of his references specifically detail the homosexual *male* prostitute.[7] The closest is a passage in which he is listing the crimes that are punishable with a death penalty. First he lists the sexual sins. "If you are guilty of pederasty, or adultery or rape of a young person, even of a female, for I need not mention the case of a male, similarly if you prostitute yourself or allow or purpose or intend any action which your age makes indecent, the penalty is death."[8] Presumably the reference to prostitution must refer to Deut. 23:17, even though the penalty for such an act is not mentioned in that biblical text.[9] Philo includes but does not single out the male prostitute, although the veiled phrase that follows against doing anything that one's age makes indecent (*aiskron*) may be pointing to the *androgynos*.

2. *Stories.* Philo shows little interest in the Bible beyond the pages of the Pentateuch and, to the best of my knowledge, he makes no reference to the story of the Levite and his concubine. In his version of Israelite history, Josephus entirely omits the events narrated in Judges 17–21. Thus the period is, as far as I know, silent about that event.

On the other hand there are frequent references to Sodom. The only allusion to it in the Greek text of *Ben Sirach* points to arrogance or pride as the root sin (16:8). The Wisdom of Solomon links it with lack of hospitality in one passage (19:13–17), and in

7. For the prohibition of prostitution, cf. Philo, *The Migration of Abraham* 224, *On Joseph* 43, *Special Laws* III. 51. All three of these, however, refer only to female prostitution. For the prohibition of Greek cults, cf. *Special Laws* I. 319.

8. Philo, *Hypothetica* 7.1. This work is extant only in fragments cited in Eusebius, *Preparatio Evangelica* VIII. 5.11 and following. The translation of Philo is that of F. H. Colson, *Philo* IX, LCL (Cambridge, Mass.: Harvard Univ. Press, 1954). In both *Migration* 224 and *Laws* III. 51 he also claims the death penalty for the prostitute.

9. As so often happens, the occasional closeness of Philo to rabbinic traditions is enticing just at this point. In the previous chapter I indicated that the rabbis interpreted Deut. 23:17 to point to secular prostitution, and that by relating the male there with the passive partner in the homosexual relation as well as with the death penalty of Lev. 20:13 they were able to say that the passive partner was guilty of the death sentence. This is identical with Philo's conclusion; whether it was also Philo's logic we shall never know.

another it stands simply as a monument to evil, caused by ignoring wisdom (10:6–8).[10]

Philo accuses the Sodomites of gluttony, lewdness, and adultery. The strongest attack, however, is directed against male homosexuality.[11] "Men mounted males without respect for the sex nature which the active partner shares with the passive."[12] The effeminate call-boy is alluded to, although the usual terms for pederasty do not appear here. Again, while Philo refers to the unnaturalness of homosexuality, he seems most concerned about the sin as the denial of procreation. He concludes with this denunciation: "Certainly, had Greeks and barbarians joined together in affecting such unions, city after city would have become a desert, as though depopulated by a pestilential sickness."[13] In another writing, which is extant only in an Armenian translation, he does apparently explicitly call the sin of Sodom pederasty.[14]

Josephus, our other narrator of the story, emphasizes the pride, arrogance, wealth, and hatred of foreigners as the reasons for God's destruction of the city.[15] Nevertheless, when he turns to the encounter of the Sodomites with Lot and the two angels, he clearly describes an intended pederastic rape, although in terms more circumspect than Philo. What is remarkable is that, in order to fit the story into the pederastic pattern which was familiar to both Josephus and his audience, he has to turn the two men (so Hebrew and Septuagint) into young men (*neaniskoi*) of remarkable beauty. "But the Sodomites, on seeing these young men of remarkably fair appearance whom Lot had taken under his roof, were bent only on violence and outrage to their youthful beauty."[16] For Hellenistic Jews, situated in urban centers where pederasty was an open phenomenon, there is no doubt about the kind of interest the Sodomites had in Lot's guests!

10. Cf. also the ambiguous references to Sodom in *Jubilees* 16.5f. and 20.5f.

11. Philo, *On Abraham* 133–41.

12. Philo, *On Abraham* 135. The translation is that of F. H. Colson, *Philo*, vol. VI, LCL (Cambridge, Mass.: Harvard Univ. Press, 1959).

13. Philo, *On Abraham* 136.

14. Philo, *Questions on Genesis* IV. 37, although the general interpretation of the Sodom story here is highly allegorical.

15. Josephus, *Antiquities* I. 194–204.

16. Josephus, *Antiquities* I. 200. The translation is that of H. J. Thackeray, *Josephus* IV, LCL (Cambridge, Mass.: Harvard Univ. Press, 1961).

3. *Homosexuality and Idolatry.* Just as certainly as had Palestinian Judaism, Hellenistic Jewish authors made no bones about the fact that pederasty was a specifically Gentile vice. This note is struck already in an early text, the *Letter of Aristeas*, which purports to describe the origin of the Greek translation of the Bible.[17] The unknown author contrasts the piety and sexual righteousness of the Jews and their law code with the activity of "the majority of other people." Among the sins of the Gentiles are male homosexuality and incest.[18]

In the Wisdom of Solomon there is a possible reference to homosexuality which, if it should prove to be the case, would signal an early linkage in Jewish thought between idolatry and homosexuality, a relationship which Paul knows and describes in Romans 1. In this treatise the author claims that idolatry is the cause of all Gentile sins. He first makes a specific reference to sexual sins: "For the beginning of sexual evil is the invention of idols."[19] Later he broadens this: "For the worship of unspeakable idols is the beginning, cause, and end of every evil."[20] In between these two references are a number of evils idolatry is said to cause. The most concentrated passage is a lengthy vice catalog in verses 25–26, which includes, but is not limited to, sexual vices. One of these is a phrase which is sometimes translated "sexual perversion" (so Revised Standard Version and New English Bible).[21] I do not myself see how the Greek can bear this translation, but if it is correct, it probably refers to homosexuality. Even should this be so, it is obvious that the text puts no particular weight on homosexuality, or any other specific sin. Seemingly, from this author's perspective, all major sins derive from worship of idols. Hence he

17. The date of the treatise is uncertain, but almost without doubt is prior to the Christian era.
18. *Letter of Aristeas* 152. Greek text ed. by H. J. Thackeray in H. Swete, *An Introduction to the Old Testament in Greek* (Cambridge: Cambridge Univ. Press, 1900), p. 545, lines 11–15.
19. Wisd. of Sol. 14:12.
20. Ibid., 14:27.
21. *Geneseōs enallagē* (v. 26). Literally the phrase could be translated "change [or: exchange] of beginning [or: generation, race, family, manner of birth]." Obviously some sort of immoral alteration of the natural is implied. If this alteration is homosexuality, however, the author has certainly phrased himself strangely and awkwardly. It should be noted, however, that the word *enallagē* (in its verbal form) does reappear in *T. Naphtali* 3.4 in reference to Sodom. Cf. the discussion in D. S. Bailey, *Homosexuality and the Western Christian Tradition* (New York and London: Longmans, Green & Co., 1955), pp. 45–48.

solves the problem of sin among Gentiles. He does not seem to have noticed the implication this might have for sins among Jews!

Under the guise of oracular utterances of ancient prophets, a Jewish literature arose which passed judgment on Gentiles and gave comfort to the Jewish community. In these writings, called *The Sibylline Oracles*, several passages refer to pagan pederasty, sometimes in relation to idol worship.[22] In one the "prediction" is made that Roman culture will permit males to draw near to males and that boys will be placed in shameful brothels.[23] In another the rise of the pious nation of the Jews is "predicted"; in contrast to pagans they will not worship idols, and shall preserve sexual purity, not "having unholy union with male children" as do many other nations (several are named explicitly).[24] God will punish these nations for this sin and for the worship of idols. Clearly sexual crime and idol worship are closely united, although it is not clear which is cause and which effect. Relationship between the two is indicated in still another passage. The reader is exhorted to flee unlawful worship and to worship the living God, to abstain from adultery, child exposure, and unceasing (or confused) intercourse with males.[25]

Another text, *The Testaments of the Twelve Patriarchs*, (if it is indeed Jewish) may possibly give further evidence of the relationship Jews felt, however they may have understood it, between idolatry and sin.[26] The patriarch Naphtali counsels his children

22. To date this collection of literature is extremely precarious. Furthermore many parts of it are seemingly by Christian authors, or have been reworked by such authors. The passages I refer to are those which scholars believe have not been influenced by Christians and which belong to the period under investigation. For discussion, cf. R. H. Charles, ed., *The Apocrypha and Pseudepigrapha of the Old Testament*, vol. 2 (Oxford: At the Clarendon Press, 1913), 368–74; Johannes Geffcken, *Komposition und Entstehungszeit der Oracula Sibyllina*, Texte und Untersuchungen 23 (Leipzig: J. C. Hinrichs'sche Buchhandlung, 1902).

23. *Sibylline Oracles* III. 185.

24. Ibid., 584–606.

25. Ibid., 762–66. A similar linkage between sin and idols is found in IV. 23–34, but the crucial line which speaks of male homosexuality is considered by authorities a later gloss. Cf. also V. 166, 386–89, and 429–31 (the last perhaps a Christian gloss).

26. Whether this long treatise is originally Jewish, Jewish but reworked by Christians, or originally Christian is a matter of great uncertainty and serious disagreement among scholars. That there are, at the least, Christian interpolations is hardly to be doubted. For a recent discussion of the issues from a rather technical perspective, cf. M. de Jonge, ed., *Studies on the Testaments of the Twelve Patriarchs* (Leiden: E. J. Brill, 1975), and H. D. Slingerland, *The Testaments of the Twelve Patriarchs: A Critical History of Research* (Missoula, Mont.: Scholars Press, 1977).

to remain true to God's will. Then abruptly he adds a warning. "Sun and moon and stars do not change their order; thus also you must not change the law of God in the disorder of your deeds. Deceived Gentiles who left the Lord changed their order and followed stones and trees, following spirits of deceit. Be not like this, my children, knowing in the firmament, earth, and in sea, and in all things made, the Lord who makes all of these, that you become not like Sodom, which changed the order of its nature. Likewise the watchers changed the order of their nature. . . ."[27] The phrase, "to change one's order," is curious and seems here equivalent to leave what is true and subvert it into a false reality.[28] For the Gentiles to change their order means to leave their proper relationship to the deity and live in a false world with false deities. To remain in true relation with the creator God is thus a defense against that changing of the order of nature which is attributed to the Sodomites. Although the phrase is strange and unparalleled in our other references to Sodom, I do not see to what other fact the author could be alluding except the homosexual inclinations of the Sodomites. If so, then *not* to change the order of relationship to God will mean *not* to violate one's heterosexual nature. The association of homosexuality with idolatry is thus well represented in Hellenistic Judaism prior to Paul.

Not surprisingly it is Philo who provides the most explicit awareness of homosexuality as a Gentile vice, although he does not bring idolatry into the discussion. I have already shown that in his treatment of the story of Sodom Philo really has the world of the present in mind.[29] In another passage he speaks fearfully of the popularity in his day of pederasty among the pagans.[30] It has invaded the cities like a troupe of disorderly revelers. Nowadays both the active and the passive partner boast of their deeds. The effeminate call-boy openly struts about with his perfume, coiffured hair, white powder and rouge on his face. "In fact the transformation of the male nature to the female is practised by

27. *T. Naphtali* 3.1–5.
28. Two different verbs are used here to denote changing. One of these also appears in Wisd. of Sol. 14:26.
29. Philo, *On Abraham* 133–41.
30. *Special Laws* III. 37–39.

them as an art and does not raise a blush."[31] He suggests such persons are honored participants in religious processions and that some even are castrated. Clearly this is an all-out attack on Gentiles. If Philo had his way, pederasts and the *androgynos* would be executed as public enemies![32]

In a still different text he ridicules the *Symposia* by Xenophon and Plato.[33] He claims that even in Plato's treatise the main point is sexual pederasty (a perverse reading, surely!). Once he has finished describing the physical, economic, spiritual, and especially the genocidal disasters of pederasty, he contrasts this Gentile evil with the sober banquets of those devoted to the pure worship of God.

In this passage he uses the typical technical terms familiar to Greek readers: "lover of boys" (*paiderastēs*), "lover" (*erastēs*), "beloved" (*erōmenos*)—although appearing in feminine because comparison is made with a girl beloved—and "favorite" (*paidika*). In addition he uses his own favorite term, *androgynos*. The kind of homosexuality he is speaking of could not be clearer. At the beginning of the section he does contrast heterosexual passion recognized by the laws of nature with that of "males for males," using the general terminology he knows from Jewish discussions; but he then immediately adds: "differing only in age." Thus he *uses* the general term, "males for males," but is so obviously *thinking* pederasty that he qualifies the general term immediately in the same sentence, and in the remainder of the discussion shows that he is moving within the world of Greco-Roman practices.

Josephus, our final witness, is much more subdued than Philo. Nevertheless he does take opportunity to suggest that some Greek cities had laws which openly promoted homosexuality (however much they have been repealed) and that they even attributed to the gods the practice of the "intercourse of males" in order to have an excuse to indulge in their unnatural pleasures (*para phusin*).[34] He also slanders Mark Anthony for his famous and undisguised lusts for boys, in the particular case mentioned by

---

31. Ibid., 37.
32. Ibid., 42.
33. Philo, *The Contemplative Life* 59–62.
34. Josephus, *Against Apion* II. 273–75.

Josephus, directed toward a member of the royal house of the Hasmoneans.[35] He has already had, as we have seen, a distinguished predecessor in this slander in Cicero himself.

4. *Homosexuality among Jews?* Faced with the public evidence of Gentile pederasty, it would have been abhorrent for the pious Hellenistic Jew to think any form of homosexuality existed in the Jewish community. Indeed, the silence of Philo and Josephus on the subject surely states loudly that they were proud of the fact that "Israel is not suspected." There is no convincing evidence to the contrary. A few passages in the *Testaments of the Twelve Patriarchs* hint that homosexuality is a reality within Judaism. Since current opinion, however, is divided over the question of the provenance of the document—whether Jewish or Christian—it is precarious to use these passages as serious evidence.[36] The *Maxims* of Pseudo-Phocylides seem to have been written by someone influenced both by Jewish and Greek wisdom. Included in this text are warnings against both male and female homosexuality.[37] Since it is not clear that the author was Jewish, and even if so, whether his maxims were directed to the Jewish community or to a larger audience, this document also cannot count as evidence.

The complete silence, or nearly so, of Jewish texts about Jewish homosexuality could lead to different conclusions. Either the greater danger felt by the Jewish minority in the Greek city led to

35. *Antiquities* XV. 25–30.
36. *T. Naphtali* 3.1—4.1 predicts that Israelites will follow after the evil of the Gentiles and the Sodomites (in the same passage which speaks of the change of order discussed above). *T. Benjamin* 9.1 predicts that Israelites will go after the (sexual) sin of Sodom and renew wantonness with women. *T. Levi* 17 predicts that even priests will become evil, and in a vice catalog listing their lusts is the word *paidophthoroi*, "corrupters of boys."
37. Pseudo-Phocylides, *Maxims*, lines 187, 190–93, 210–16. See the translation by B. S. Easton, "Pseudo-Phocylides," *Anglican Theological Review* 14 (1932): 222–28. In *The Book of the Secrets of Enoch*, extant only in two late Slavic traditions, there occurs in *one* of the traditions two references to homosexuality as meriting God's eternal punishment in hell (vividly described). The references for these passages are 10.4 and 34.2 in the edition of Morfill and Charles. Problems concerning which tradition is earlier and the possible origin and dating of the original writing are so enormously complicated, however, that it is useless to include the texts in our study or to pursue the difficult issues. Fortunately there is nothing in these passages which adds anything to our knowledge. One might wish to consult W. R. Morfill and R. H. Charles, *The Book of the Secrets of Enoch* (Oxford: At the Clarendon Press, 1896) in comparison with A. Vaillant, *Le Livre des Secrets d' Henoch* (Paris: Institut d' Etudes Slaves, 1952).

stringent measures of rejection and protection, or the contrast continually made between the sexual purity of the Jews and the impurity of the rest of the world effectively silenced evidence to the contrary. All that can really be said is that Hellenistic Jewish authors write as if such practices were unheard of within the community.

SUMMARY

Since the above evidence has been marshaled in terse and rather uninterpreted fashion, it may be helpful here to summarize the results of our discussion about Hellenistic Judaism.

1. *Practices.* Homosexuality is discussed as a male vice. With the exception of the one reference in Pseudo-Phocylides, there is no reference to female homosexuality. Male homosexuality is described as pederasty, either explicitly or implicitly. Pederasty is said to exist only among Gentiles.

2. *Attitudes.* Uncompromisingly the judgment is negative. Homosexuality is evil. There are three reasons given for this. (*a*) It is against nature, although, perhaps surprisingly, the statements to this effect are not as strong or as explicit as in Greco-Roman literature. (*b*) It denies procreation as the divinely appointed aim of intercourse. This judgment is made only by Philo, but with him is strongly stated. (*c*) As one sin among many, but perhaps particularly noted because it was seen as a vice unique to pagans, homosexuality is related to idolatry. In some unexplained way, idolatry leads to sexual perversion of all sorts.

3. *Language.* The Septuagint gives faithful translations of the laws in Leviticus, providing words that may be the origin of the rare word *arsenokoitēs*. While Jewish authors may use general terms found in Leviticus of "male" and "man," it is obvious that when they attack pagan practices they are attacking pederasty.

4. *Comparison with Palestinian Judaism.* (*a*) *Similarities.* Both have little interest in the subject, but where it surfaces both are unalterably opposed. Both virtually ignore female homosexuality. Both attack homosexuality as a Gentile vice. Both ground their opposition in the common constitution, the Bible. (*b*) *Differences.* (1) Language. Palestinian Judaism remains content, by and large, to use

the terminology of the Bible; Hellenistic Judaism uses both biblical and Greco-Roman terminology. This is especially the case with Philo. (2) Arguments. Palestinian Judaism did not, apparently, feel the need to show arguments *why* homosexuality is wrong. The fact that the Bible legislates against it is sufficient cause for opposition. Hellenistic Judaism mounts a few arguments, although in comparison with like-minded opponents in pagan culture, these arguments are few. The only argument that Hellenistic Jews perhaps borrowed from the modern culture is that homosexuality is contrary to nature. Perhaps ultimately both Hellenistic and Palestinian Jews felt the judgment so obvious that little or no refutation was needed.

7

The Early Church:
Echoes of a Tradition

Today's denominational debates about homosexuality revolve around the pronouncements in the New Testament. Granted, the laws in Leviticus are unequivocally opposed to male homosexual activity. Since the Old Testament is emphatic about many issues ignored or discarded by the Christian churches, however, it cannot be said that the Old Testament alone would control contemporary decisions, were it not for the fact that the New Testament repeats these negative judgments. Nor, it would seem, do post-biblical judgments and attitudes of Christian thinkers figure in any prominent way in the debate. This seems to hold true, in some quarters, for psychological as well as theological assessments. It is the Christian *Canon* which is frequently invoked as the final and single authority, and this for both practical *and* theological purposes means the New Testament itself. Particularly for those who view the Christian *Canon* as the only and ultimate authority it becomes absolutely essential to understand the import of the relevant New Testament passages and, as has been repeatedly emphasized in this book, to grasp just what is being opposed.

In comparison with the abundance of materials about pederasty in Greco-Roman literature, the New Testament is virtually silent. In my judgment it cannot be said that the early church was nearly as interested in the moral issues pertaining to the practices as was Greco-Roman society as a whole. For the churches which produced the Gospels, homosexuality was obviously not an issue at all; there is not a single statement about it in any of these writings.[1] The Book of Acts certainly and the Revelation of John most probably do not mention it.[2] Only in the epistolary literature does the issue explicitly emerge, and at that only three times.[3]

Paul refers twice to it, and in a writing identified by scholars as composed later than Paul, although in his name, it is mentioned once.[4] In two of these three, homosexuality is mentioned only in passing. Only in one (Rom. 1:26–27) is the topic integrated into the larger discussion which the author is pursuing. Furthermore,

1. Sodom is mentioned a few times, but never in connection with homosexuality. In Matt. 10:15 (Luke 10:12; 'Q'), Sodom symbolizes attitudes toward hospitality. In Matt. 11:23–24, it is used as a foil to talk about repentance. In Luke 17:29, the destruction of Sodom symbolizes the suddenness with which the eschaton will occur. On the difficulties in imagining what Jesus' own attitudes might have been, cf. the discussion in Tom Horner, *Jonathan Loved David: Homosexuality in Biblical Times* (Philadelphia: Westminster Press, 1978), pp. 110–26.

2. In Rev. 11:8 Sodom is one of the names given to Jerusalem as a term of opprobrium (already in Isa. 1:10). Two other words, both in vice lists (21:8; 22:15), have on occasion been taken to point to homosexuals. The terms are so general, however, that it is impossible to know whether they hint at the practices or not. To discuss them here would not add anything to our picture. Cf. the analysis in D. S. Bailey, *Homosexuality and the Western Christian Tradition* (New York and London: Longmans, Green & Co., 1955), pp. 41–45.

3. There are two other closely related passages which scholars have often interpreted as referring to judgments on homosexual practices: Jude 6—13 and 2 Pet. 2:4–18. The authors of these writings (2 Peter is widely held to be literarily dependent on Jude) are attacking Christians whom they believe to be guilty of unethical conduct as well as theological heresy. The misconduct seems to be sexual in character, but the language used is so elusive as to make any certain judgment impossible. What triggers possible reference to homosexual misconduct is the reference in both to Sodom and Gomorrah. Since, however, the reference to this story is closely attached to the Jewish legend (suggested by Gen. 6:4) of angels cohabiting with human women, the "pursuing after strange flesh" surely relates primarily to the Sodomites' lust after the "men" who were actually angels. This is the view of Kelly in his very careful exegesis (J. N. D. Kelly, *The Epistles of Peter and of Jude* [New York: Harper & Row, 1969], pp. 258f). At the same time he suggests that "it is probably legitimate (see on [Jude] 8) to infer that he is snidely accusing the innovators of homosexual practices" (p. 259). This is a possible, but not necessary judgment, and the author of 2 Peter, by speaking of adulterous lust (2:14) seems to give the whole attack a heterosexual direction. What is remarkable is that, whatever the sexual misconduct really was, both authors associate it with the agape meals of the Christian communities, as if the people attacked had turned these presumably religious meals into a secular banquet in which sexual encounters were sought. *If* the passage in Jude should accuse these Christians of homosexual lust, then the agape meals had, in his view, been turned into affairs in which pederastic interest became manifest.

4. 1 Tim. 1:10. Of all the writings attributed to Paul which have the greatest claim to be deutero-Pauline, the Pastorals (1 and 2 Timothy, and Titus) are at the top of the list. Probably 1 Timothy was written toward the beginning of the second century C.E.

in all three of these passages the material is expressed in very traditional terms, that of Greco-Roman and/or Hellenistic Jewish cultures. Thus not only is the New Testament church uninterested in the topic, it has nothing new to say about it. The passage in Romans may on the surface seem to be an exception to this judgment, but in the final analysis I do not think such a claim can be substantiated.

On the other hand, it can hardly be accidental that the three passages are addressed to churches located in the Greco-Roman world where pederasty was the norm for homosexual relationships.[5] Thus it must be a beginning presupposition that these passages all oppose one form or another of pederasty, insofar as they speak of male homosexuality. But it is now time to investigate carefully these three statements.

1 CORINTHIANS 6:9–10

This passage is the first in Christian literature to refer to homosexuality:

> Do you not know that the unrighteous will not inherit the kingdom of God? Do not be deceived; neither the immoral, nor idolaters, nor adulterers, nor *malakoi*, nor *arsenokoitai*, nor thieves, nor the greedy, nor drunkards, nor revilers, nor robbers will inherit the kingdom of God.

I have left the two key terms untranslated, since they are by now familiar to the reader. Before we consider their possible meaning in this particular passage, however, it is crucial to determine its literary form and the larger context in which it is embedded.

1. *Form and Function.* Scholars have nicknamed the form exhibited here the "catalog of vices," for the obvious reasons that we have here a *list* of evil habits or attitudes, strung together in rather loose fashion with no clear logic manifested about the choice or order of the particular vices in the list. This form was popular in Greco-Roman literature of the day, including that of

---

5. Corinth and Rome. 1 Timothy cannot be geographically pinpointed but is certainly aimed at the Gentile world. The makeup of the churches at Rome and Corinth, according to Paul himself, seems to have been largely of former pagans.

Hellenistic Judaism. We have already noted such a catalog in the Wisdom of Solomon, in a section that scores the Gentiles for idolatry.[6] Paul obviously likes the form because he uses it several times throughout his writings.[7]

What is clear is that the users or creators of these lists do not carefully select the individual items to fit the context with which they are dealing. The lists were often, apparently, traditional. What was important was the list as list, and perhaps its length. The more vices included, the greater the impression on the reader. That is, the list was a club used to hit an opponent over the head or to warn the writer's own community of the penalty for evil living. Any relation between an individual item in a list and the situation addressed was thus, more often than not, nonexistent. Furthermore, the items might well be partially, at least, memorized from a traditional stock of evils.

The implications for any particular item, in relation to author and context, are twofold. One, it cannot be known what weight any individual author gave to any specific vice listed. Two, it cannot be known whether any specific item really fits the context for which the catalog is being used. Thus what Paul cites in 1 Cor. 6:9–10 is a stereotyped literary form, which may or may not reflect his own sense of priorities, either in general or with regard to the specific situation of the Corinthian church.

2. *Context.* We have now clarified the *function* such a catalog in general had for its author. Now the question must be raised, how the catalog functions in our particular context.

The first thing to note is that there are really *three* catalogs in this section, which spans 1 Corinthians 5 and 6. This larger section is very carefully constructed. Paul's intent is to attack the church for certain practices he has heard are taking place. There are three: (1) a man living with his father's former wife (5:1–5), (2) church members going to civil courts against each other, when

6. Wis. of Sol. 14:25–26. One finds such catalogs everywhere. E.g., Maximus of Tyre XVIII. 84b; XIX 90a; *Sibylline Oracles* III. 36–39; Epictetus II. 16.45. Philo even has one that contains 147 vices! Cf. *Sacrifices of Abel and Cain* 32.

7. Gal. 5:19–21; 1 Cor. 5:10–11; 6:9–10; 2 Cor. 12:20; Rom. 1:29–31; 13:13. There were corresponding catalogs of virtues. In Paul they are found at Gal. 5:22–23; 2 Cor. 6:6; Phil. 4:8. Both kinds of catalogs are found elsewhere in the New Testament.

they ought, thinks Paul, to set up their own ecclesiastical court (6:1–8), and (3) church members going to female prostitutes (6:12–20). Obviously, homosexuality is not an issue; the sexual sins are heterosexual.

Underlying Paul's displeasure is his basic concern for the purity of the community. He urges the church to cleanse out the old leaven (here a symbol for impurity), to exclude sinful members from church fellowship, exhorts them to consider, whatever their former sins as pagans, that they have been washed and cleansed, and to think of themselves as a holy temple for the Spirit of God. The specific sins are not so much in and of themselves important; they become an issue because they are manifestations of the staining of the purity of the church. *This in turn indicates what the function of the catalogs is in the context.* They serve as a foil to create the contrast between former impurity and present (desired) purity and to serve as a warning of the consequences of sinful living, of allowing further impurity into the community.

The three catalogs in this section are carefully and closely related. The first contains four vices; the second, six, with all of the first four included; the third, ten, with all of the previous six included. Thus the second adds two to the list; the third adds four. Below are the lists with the vices in the order in which they occur. (The italicized vices are the new ones inserted into the lists.)

1 COR. 5:10	1 COR. 5:11	1 COR. 6:9–10
immoral	immoral	immoral
greedy	greedy	idolators
robbers	idolaters	*adulterers*
idolaters	*revilers*	*malakoi*
	drunkards	*arsenokoitai*
	robbers	*thieves*
		greedy
		drunkards
		revilers
		robbers

The first conclusion is obvious: as the lists grow in length, the size of the club increases. Paul is building toward a rhetorical climax. The beginning and end of that final, most intense list is sig-

naled by the warning that such deeds exclude one from the kingdom of God. The warning could not be clearer, however much
one suspects Paul to be engaging in a certain hyperbole. He then
points his finger at the Corinthians' pre-Christian life, "and some
of you did these things" (au. trans.) (6:11*a*). Yet this is graciously
assumed by the Apostle to be a past life, and he ends with the
concession that "you have been washed, you have been sanctified,
you have been justified in the name of the Lord Jesus Christ and
in the Holy Spirit of our God" (au. trans.) (6:11*b*).

The second conclusion is equally clear: Paul does not care about
any specific item in the lists. There is no indication he wished to
emphasize one or more vices. One might think that the four
which appear in all of the catalogs might have special import for
him, but even this is doubtful. In the *first* place, the order of these
four varies from list to list. Only the "immoral" item consistently
retains its place as first. In fact, in the first list, the Greek suggests
that "greedy" and "robbers" are pointing to the same kind of vice,
since they are syntactically linked more closely together than any
words in the lists.[8] Yet in both the following lists the two words
are widely separated by other items. The linkage in list one is thus
purely rhetorical. In the *second* place, the third list adds a word
translated here "thieves"; scholars, however, do not see any sub-
stantive difference from the word translated "robbers." All this
can only mean that Paul is using traditional items, with no particular item of special significance to him. It goes without saying, of
course, that he disapproves of all such activities.

Paul is quite aware that he is addressing former pagans. One
might thus conclude that he lists here specific vices which he asso-
ciates with dissolute pagan life. One could then consider important the threefold use of "idolater" and certainly the sexual sins,
including the vices indicated by *malakoi* and *arsenokoitai*. This possibility needs to be considered. Yet even here caution is needed.
In Rom. 2:17–22 Paul accuses Jews of thievery and adultery, two
words in common with the third list in Corinthians. "While you
preach against stealing, do you steal? You who say that one must
not commit adultery, do you commit adultery?" (vv. 21–22*a*).

---

8. Literally the Greek would read: "Not at all [meaning] the immoral of this
world, *or* the greedy *and* robbers, *or* idolaters." A disjunctive particle separates the
items except greedy and robbers which are joined together by a conjunction.

Then he adds a curious finale: "You who abhor idols, do you rob temples?" (v. 22*b*). This is a strange and difficult charge. "To rob temples" could be taken literally, in which case Paul probably sees Jews desecrating pagan temples in the name of monotheism. The word has, however, also a more general meaning: "to be sacrilegious." In any case, the parallelism of these sentences indicates that Paul senses that in the act of "robbing temples" the Jew is really violating his principle of rejecting idols.

A further reason for caution in applying the vice list in Corinthians too explicitly to Gentile vices is comparison with another vice list addressed to former pagans. In the extensive list in Gal. 5:19–21 (fifteen items), there are only two in common with 1 Cor. 6:9–10—idolatry and drunkenness. It is not unimportant to note that *malakoi* and *arsenokoitai* are absent from Galatians. The conclusion that presses for acceptance is that very little connection can be drawn between *any* vice list in Paul and the context of the passage.

3. *Relation to traditional lists.* This utter lack of relationship is all the more reason that one must ask the question: To what extent is Paul leaning on preformed tradition in these lists, and to which source(s) must one ascribe such tradition, if it be found? If there is dependence on such tradition, it must surely be the third list which is dependent. The brevity of the first two would not suggest a unit lengthy enough to count. That would mean that, in point of fact, Paul is beginning in his thinking with the third list and excerpts from that list to create the first two.

One clue that the third list is traditional is the appearance at beginning and end of the phrase, "inherit the kingdom of God." The kingdom of God is a notion embedded in Jewish apocalyptic, and "to inherit the kingdom of God" is familiar to any reader of the Gospels. Yet in Hellenistic Judaism and in Hellenistically-oriented early Christian tradition, especially that represented by the epistolary literature in the New Testament, this notion is not prominent. Paul is no exception.[9] That this list is bracketed in an important way by the phrase, not common to Paul, may certainly

9. "Kingdom of God" points to the eschatological, future reign of God over all the world or over the saints in heaven. The phrase is found in Paul elsewhere only in Rom. 14:17, 1 Cor. 4:20; 15:24; 15:50; Gal. 5:21, 1 Thess. 2:12, and (if it is authentically Paul) 2 Thess. 1:5. The verb "to reign," in the eschatological sense, is used in 1 Cor. 4:8 and 15:25.

suggest that Paul is here dependent on a list already preformed in Palestinian Judaism and mediated by Hellenistic Judaism or Christianity. Furthermore, the very appearance of the word *arsenokoitai*, if our derivation of it is correct, indicates some contact with Hellenistic Judaism. These arguments thus suggest the likelihood that the entire list in 1 Cor. 6:9–10 is borrowed from earlier, Hellenistic Jewish tradition.

4. The words *malakoi* and *arsenokoitai*. It should by now be clear that Paul gives no particular weight to these words, nor is he especially concerned to accuse former pagans in his churches of the kind of homosexuality encompassed in these terms; otherwise they would certainly have appeared in the catalog in Galatians and perhaps elsewhere as well.

Malakos. This word has been sufficiently examined above and there a twofold conclusion was drawn. First, the word, literally meaning soft and by extension "effeminate," in no way ever assumed a technical status referring to pederastic relations or persons. Second, by association, however, the word occurs in several texts *pointing in pejorative ways* to the "call-boy," the youth who consciously imitated feminine styles and ways and who walked the thin line between passive homosexual activity for pleasure and that for pay. Used in association with another more explicit term or within a context of pederasty, it would clearly point to such a person and always in a negative way. That is, in sexual contexts it is never a neutral term.

Malakos would, thus, carry a weight in a catalog of vices which terms more neutral in the vocabulary of sexuality would not. Furthermore, it would refer to a specific dimension of pederasty which, as we have seen, neither proponent nor opponent of pederasty ever defended. It is not pederasty as such which is pointed to by *malakos* but only a specific and detested form of it.

Arsenokoitēs. While *malakos* is ambiguous to a greater or lesser extent, the word *arsenokoitēs* has always seemed more straightforwardly to express a homosexual act. As already suggested, it is made up of two words, *arsen*=male, and *koitē*=bed, then marriage-bed, then sexual intercourse in general. As frequently happens in Greek, the emphasis or action is expressed by the second part of the compound, which may have, as it seems here, verbal force. The first word of the compound can be taken as the *object* of the second part. If these fit our word here, then the second part can most easily be translated as a participle and connected to the first by a preposition: "lying (with) a male," or, turned into a noun, "one who lies with a male."[10]

Nevertheless, the term is strange. As far as I have been able to determine, its earliest extant occurrence is in 1 Cor. 6:10.[11] Apparently, then, *it has no recoverable history prior to Paul's use of it.* This opens the way to at least two different directions of interpretation, or reinterpretation.

Since there is no series of already established usages which determine what the word *has* to mean in 1 Corinthians, it is conceivable that later interpretations of the word are incorrect, especially so since the word does not appear after 1 Corinthians with any frequency. Recently John Boswell has argued that the first word in the compound is the subject rather than the object. The definition thus would be derived from the sense, "a male lying," that is, a male having intercourse. This would point to a fornicator, or more specifically to a male prostitute, who services women and/or men.[12]

2. The second direction is the one already proposed in this book. If the word has no prehistory in Greek literature—and I am certain that it does not appear in the Greek pagan discussions of pederasty we have analyzed in previous chapters—then its origin and meaning may be sought in another language. That is, the word may be a translation of a foreign term or phrase.

I have argued above that in early rabbinic legal discussions, the

10. The lexicons give the gender of the noun as masculine, but since this first appearance of the word occurs in the plural, there is no *grammatical* reason why it could not be a feminine noun (in this declension feminine and masculine nouns have the same plural ending), referring to a woman who sleeps (around?) with males, cf. also John Boswell, *Christianity, Social Tolerance, and Homosexuality* (Chicago: Univ. of Chicago Press, 1980), p. 345, n. 27.

11. According to T. Nägeli (*Der Wortschatz des Apostels Paulus* [Göttingen: Vandenhoeck & Ruprecht, 1905] p. 46), the word first appears in the poets of imperial times. His instances, however, are late. The earliest occurrence is probably the one in *Sibylline Oracles* II. 73, a work of uncertain time and provenance, but stemming from a Jewish or early Christian author. Almost certainly 1 Corinthians is earlier than the second book of the *Sibylline Oracles*. Cf., also Boswell, *Christianity, Social Tolerance, and Homosexuality*, p. 341, n. 17.

12. Cf. the learned discussion in Boswell, *Christianity, Social Tolerance, and Homosexuality*, pp. 341–53.

term most often used to describe male homosexuality is *mishkav zakur*, "lying with a male."[13] *Arsenokoitēs* can then be seen as a literal translation of the Hebrew phrase. We have also seen that the parts of the Greek compound appear in the Septuagint versions of the laws in Leviticus. This provides the Greek linguistic link between the rabbinic phrase and the term in the vice catalog in 1 Corinthians. Thus the word *arsenokoitēs* originated in Hellenistic-Jewish circles as an attempt to translate the rabbinic quasi-legal term into understandable Greek, perhaps with the deliberate intention of avoiding contact with the usual Greek terminology.[14]

If this is correct, then the first word of the compound is the object, not subject, of the action, and the usual interpretation of its meaning is seen to be correct. Furthermore, since in rabbinic discussion the *mishkav zakur* is the active, not the passive partner, it would function in the same way in its Greek version, denoting the adult, who took the active role in the sexual encounter. But to what kind of role and what kind of relationship does it point?

In and of itself the word does not help answer that question, but seen in relationship to *malakos*, the issue becomes clarified. If the *malakos* points to the effeminate call-boy, then the *arsenokoitēs* in this context must be the active partner who keeps the *malakos* as a "mistress" or who hires him on occasion to satisfy his sexual desires. No more than *malakos* is to be equated with the youth in general, the *erōmenos*, can *arsenokoitēs* be equated with the adult in general, the *erastēs*. A very specific dimension of pederasty is being denounced with these two terms. Seen in this way, the list shares the disapproval of this form of pederasty in agreement with the entire literature of the Greco-Roman world on the topic![15]

13. Cf. p. 83 above. If it is a coinage of Hellenistic Jews taken from rabbinic discussions, this would fully explain what Boswell finds so remarkable, that the word does not appear in Greco-Roman discussions of pederasty, and that in later patristic authors, the word is either avoided or given other meanings. To a native-speaking Greek, without contact with Jewish debate, the word would have made little sense.

14. It is possible, of course, that Paul is responsible for the term. Since, however, he seems quite uninterested in the issue, and since the list seems quite traditional, it is more likely that he is using a term already known in circles of Hellenistic Jews acquainted with rabbinic discussions.

15. This is also the specific dimension of pederasty that Philo attacks so vehemently. E.g., *Special Laws* III. 37–39; *Contemplative Life* 59–62.

Since the above discussion has bordered on the tedious, a quick summary is perhaps justified. The list in 1 Cor. 6:9–10 is traditional and bears no relationship to any specific recoverable context within the Corinthian situation. There is absolutely no indication that Paul is putting stress on any items in the lists, let alone those which occur only once in the full form in vv. 9–10. *Malakos* and *arsenokoitēs* occur because they are part of the fund of the catalog on which Paul is dependent. The words point to a very specific form of pederasty, one the entire literature agrees is evil.

The words cannot be said to point to or exclude the general practice of homosexuality from the kingdom of God. Female homosexuality is not included under these terms. The generic model of pederasty is not attacked, only the specific form described above. If we would hold up an example of what these words attack, then we should remember the dissolute and degenerate Timarchus, the number of adults who bought him or kept him for hire, and their own jealousies and quarrels. Nothing could be further from the model aspired to by the gay community today.

ROMANS 1:26–27

The major reference to homosexuality in the New Testament (all two verses!) is found in a carefully crafted section of Romans (1:18–32). Here, as we shall see, Paul has a major *theological* goal in mind; ethical concerns or admonitions lie far from his purpose.

> Therefore, God gave them up to dishonorable passions. For not only did their females exchange natural intercourse for that which is against nature, but also males, leaving natural intercourse with females, lusted in their desire for one another, males working shame with males and receiving the punishment within themselves which their falsehood necessitated (au. trans.).

These verses are so composed of commonplaces of Greek and Jewish attitudes toward homosexuality that, as the reader must see instantly, there is hardly a word which one could not find in similar passages we have inspected in previous chapters. It is completely informed by Hellenistic Jewish propaganda against Gentiles, a propaganda that had apparently absorbed arguments from the Greeks themselves.[16]

Nevertheless, this passage is integrated into the Pauline argument in a decisive way, something which was not the case with the glancing reference to the "call-boy" in 1 Cor. 6:9. Furthermore, as we shall see, this larger argument depends in part on the Hellenistic Jewish claim that homosexuality is closely related to idolatry. Thus, just as in the passage in Corinthians it is crucial to analyze first the larger context.

1. *Theological context.* The overarching theme of Paul in Romans is the justice and mercy of God as revealed from the perspective of the Christ event.[17] The ultimate goal of his theme is 11:32: "For God has shut up all people into disobedience that he may have mercy upon all" (au. trans.). The penultimate goal, however, is 3:19*b*: "That every mouth may be silenced and the entire world held accountable to God" (au. trans.). The argument could be summarized in one sentence: Since the entire world, both Jew and Gentile, is guilty of sin, grace (salvation) is entirely God's gift and extends equally to Jew and Gentile.

But how does he come to the conclusion that sin is universal? In other words, what is his story of the fall of humankind? While the reader might immediately jump to the conclusion that the fall must have to do with Adam and the stories in Genesis 2–3, Paul does not come to that topic until Romans 5, in which he is more interested in contrasting Adam with Christ than using the Adam story to prove the fallenness of humanity.[18]

I would suggest, to the contrary, that Paul's real story of the universal fall is narrated in Rom. 1:18–32. Most scholars believe that vv. 18–32 refer only to the fall of the Gentiles, while the sin of the Jews is not mentioned until Romans 2. There is no opportunity here to argue the issue, but it seems to me that in Romans 1

16. The notions that homosexuality is dishonorable, shameful, that it is against nature, the phrase "males with males"—all these we have seen repeatedly in the previous chapters.

17. For an analysis of the theological logic of Paul in Romans, cf. R. Scroggs, "Paul as Rhetorician: Two Homilies in Romans 1–11," in *Jews, Greeks and Christians: Essays in Honor of William David Davies*, edited by R. Hamerton-Kelly and R. Scroggs (Leiden: E. J. Brill, 1976), pp. 271–98.

18. Cf. R. Scroggs, *The Last Adam: A Study in Pauline Anthropology* (Philadelphia: Fortress Press, 1966), pp. 75–82.

Paul is speaking of a universal fall, or deception, which includes Jews as well as Gentiles. In Romans 2 Paul will attempt to demonstrate to the Jews that they also belong to that fall, however little they realize it.[19]

> For the wrath of God is revealed from heaven against all ungodliness and wickedness of people who by their wickedness *suppress the truth.* For what can be *known* about God is *plain* to them, because God has *shown* it to them. Ever since the creation of the world his invisible nature, namely his eternal power and deity, *has been clearly perceived* in the things that have been made. So they are without excuse; for although they *knew* God they did not honor him as God or give thanks to him, but they *became futile in their thinking* and their *unfit minds were darkened.* Claiming to be *wise,* they became *fools,* and exchanged the glory of the immortal God for images resembling mortal humans or birds or animals or reptiles. (Rom. 1:18–23; au. trans.)

The language of mental and moral perception and evaluation of what is true as over against what is false is pervasive in these sentences (cf. the italicized words). The real fall of humankind is its refusal (the issue here is "willful ignorance") to acknowledge and be obedient to the true God. Ultimately that means the refusal to acknowledge the true reality in its entirety, for the refusal to "know" God brings in its turn a false knowledge of the entire creation, including a false knowledge of the human self. In short, to "fall" is to refuse to live in the true world and to construct a false world in its stead—all the while thinking, believing, and claiming that the false constructed reality is actually true. Thus "sinners" are those who live in this falsehood but who claim it (think it) to be true. Hence Paul can say at the end of Romans 1 (v. 32): "They not only do these things [act falsely] but approve of [others] who do them" (au. trans.). They are in agreement that their world is true and good and beautiful and can—will—not

---

19. Cf. M. Hooker, "Adam in Romans I," *New Testament Studies* 6 (1959/60): 297–306, J. Jervell, *Imago Dei* (Göttingen: Vandenhoeck & Ruprecht, 1960), pp. 312–31, and Scroggs, *Last Adam,* p. 75, n. 3. Jews are equally sinners with Gentiles (Rom. 3:9–20, and while they have a zeal for God it is informed by ignorance (Rom. 10:2–3). Cf. also 2 Cor. 3:12–15. Jews live under bondage to the same powers and principalities that enslave Gentiles (Gal. 4:8–9) when they live under the law. And if the language about idolatry in Rom. 1:23 is related to an interpretation of the idolatry of the golden calf (cf. Ps. 106:19–20), then Israel is implicated in idolatry just as in ignorance.

perceive that it is in fact false and based on false premises (false gods).

While this may seem to exclude the Jews from such judgment, since they worship the true God, from Paul's perspective it does not. One major argument in Romans is, in fact, that the Jews do not really know God, that is, do not know what God desires and has in mind for humankind. Only in and through the Christ event can this willful ignorance, whether from Jew or Gentile, be transformed into true perception and thus true obedience.[20]

One traditional source of this "story" of the fall is the Jewish argument we have already encountered, that idolatry brings with it false and evil acts. The claim in Wisdom of Solomon can be repeated here: "For the worship of idols not to be named is the beginning and cause and end of every evil" (14:27). Paul has, it seems to me, so transformed this judgment in his thinking that it becomes a profound basis for the understanding of the tragedy of human history and its sinfulness, including the history of the Jews. Paul does not trivialize the argument by harping on the ridiculousness of worshiping sticks and stones (as the Wisdom of Solomon tends to do). Rather he moves behind the outward manifestation to the deepest cause of idolatry, namely that refusal to acknowledge the true, sovereign God, which refusal brings in its turn, false gods, false world, false self-awareness, and false perspectives on human activity.

2. *Ethical results of living in the false world.* From this basic theological affirmation he then moves to give what he considers to be illustrations of the results of living in that false world. Even these illustrations, however, are given theological depth by Paul's claim that false living is actually both *sign* (to those who have been restored to true knowledge) and *reality* of God's judgment upon that world which has forsaken him. Living in falsehood *is* the manifestation of the wrath of God. And since for Paul "wrath" is a term for eschatological judgment, and since this wrath is a present manifestation, Paul is saying that living and acting in that false

20. In Rom. 1:28 the mind of humanity is said to be "unfit," i.e., unable to function as an agent of true perception (*adokimos*). In Rom. 12:2, Paul exhorts the believers: "Do not be conformed to this world, but be transformed by the *renewal of your mind*, that you may test out and find (*dokimadzo*) what is the will of God, what is good and pleasing, and perfect" (au. trans.).

world is in itself God's sentence of doom. To live in that false reality is all the hell one could need. Of course the complete irony is that it is precisely those living in that world who do not "know" that they are, in fact, living in hell.

The human results, or illustrations of the results, are given in three parallel sentences, each introduced by the phrase, "God gave them up," in relation to three distinct dimensions of human existence, heart (body), passions (emotions) and mind.

Therefore God gave them up in the desires of their *hearts* to impurity, to the dishonoring of their *bodies* among themselves.

Therefore God gave them up to dishonorable *passions*; [then follow the sentences about homosexuality].

And since they did not see fit to hold to God in knowledge, God gave them up to an unfit *mind*, to do things not appropriate, being filled with all unrighteousness—evil, covetousness, malice, full of envy, murder, strife, deceit, malignity, gossips, slanderers, haters of God, insolent, haughty, boastful, inventors of evil, disobedient to parents, foolish, faithless, heartless, ruthless.

Though they know God's decree that those who do such things deserve to die, they not only do them but approve those who practice them.

Three points of clarification need to be made. The *first* is that the phrase, "God gave them up," means that people now living in the false reality do what they choose. God does not force them into such false actions; his judgment lies in his leaving them where they want to be, in actions which, as already suggested, they think to be good and right. This is the ultimate irony of their fate. The *second* is that Paul heaps up anthropological terms— heart, body, passions, mind—apparently to indicate that this false reality permeates a person's entire existence. All dimensions of one's self are distorted by the false reality in which he or she lives.

The *third* relates to the use of illustrations Paul chooses. The structure of the passage shows that for heart-body Paul gives no illustration. That which illustrates passion (emotions) is a traditional Hellenistic Jewish judgment on homosexuality. For the third, the unfit mind (i.e., that which cannot judge between what is true and what is false), Paul inserts the most detailed and vigorous vice catalog in all his letters. That the two illustrations are traditional units need not be belabored at this stage of our investigation. This suggests a further point, equally clear it seems to me. The illustrations do not necessarily fit one part of the self more than another. For instance, the illustration of homosexuality could as easily have gone under the first part—the dishonoring of body. The vice catalog is so all-inclusive it could have fitted as well under either the first or second part as under the third. Paul again seems to be conforming to his rhetorical instincts, each successive section having a greater intensity. The first has no illustration; the second, one specific vice; the third, an impressive and culminating list of all sorts of vices.

The conclusion to be drawn is that the illustrations are secondary to his basic theological structure. Paul is not primarily concerned here to attack specific vices; he uses the illustrations to point up his main theological argument. This does not, of course, imply that Paul is not judging homosexuality, but it does suggest that the Apostle is not "out to get them," as some people have assumed.

With the above qualification in mind, we can now turn to an interpretation of vv. 26–27. "For not only did their females exchange natural intercourse for that which is against nature. . . . " Taken independently of the following verse, it would not be certain that this clause referred to female homosexuality at all. Indeed some have suspected it could refer to various positions of heterosexual intercourse deemed deviate by pious Jews.[21] It could as well be hinting at artificial phalli which we know were used by women of the day to stimulate themselves—although such stimulation could take place in the context of homosexual encounters. Since the following verse is without question an attack on male homosexuality, however, and since the two verses are so closely linked in the Greek, it is virtually certain that Paul and the tradition on which he is dependent had lesbianism in mind.

Only two features call for notice here. The first is that the use of the "argument from nature" is a commonplace of Greco-Roman attack on pederasty and has nothing to do with any theories of natural law or with interpretation of the Genesis stories of cre-

21. Cf. the evidence and discussion in Paul Billerbeck, *Kommentar zum Neuen Testament aus Talmud und Midrasch,* vol. 3 (Munich: Col. Beck'sche, 1926), pp. 68f.

ation. Indeed, the phrase translated "that which is against nature" is that Greek which we have encountered over and over again, *para phusin*. The second is that female homosexuality is mentioned at all! This is remarkable given the fact that in both Jewish and Greco-Roman discussions, that topic is virtually absent. Since there are no Old Testament laws prohibiting female homosexuality, why does Paul include it here? If Paul is dependent on a pre-formed tradition for these two verses, he of course found it in that tradition. Why the tradition included it is a question to which I see no answer. But why *Paul* included it may well be his insistence that the false world is lived in equally by women as well as men (just as there is equality between sexes in the world of the new creation). Hence his illustrations must be inclusive of both sexes.

The verse about male homosexuality is more elaborate and intense. "But also males leaving natural intercourse with females lusted in their desires for one another, males working shame with males and receiving the punishment within themselves which their falsehood necessitated." The first point to make here is the obvious one that Paul uses the Jewish form of expression, male with male, as in Leviticus, without further specification. This does not mean, however, that he would have anything in mind other than pederasty, any more than Philo, who can use the "male and male" terminology when he is explicitly referring to pederasty.[22] The second is the appearance again, if less explicitly, of the argument from nature: males leave the natural (*phusikēn*) intercourse with females for lust for other males (thus, implicitly, against nature). Thirdly, this works shame (*askemosunē*), a typical, negative Greek judgment on pederasty.[23] Finally, the ambiguous last phrase calls for attention: "Receiving the punishment (literally reward) within themselves which their falsehood necessitated." There have been two interpretations. Either Paul is hinting at physical disease (perhaps venereal) which homosexual intercourse could cause, or he counts the distortion of homosexuality itself as

22. Philo, *Contemplative Life* 59–62.
23. The same root in Plutarch *Erōtikos* 751E. Cf. related words (*aiskunomai* or *aiskron* families) in Demosthenes, *Erōtikos* 5; Andocides I. 100; Dio Chrysostom 7. 133; Plato, *Symposium* 182A; Pseudo-Lucian, *Erōtes* 21, 24, 28; Pseudo-Lucian, *Dialogues of the Courtesans* 292; Xenophon, *Memorabilia* I. vi. 13.

the punishment. The latter seems to me most likely, given the reference in that phrase to the false reality in which people now live.

3. *Conclusion.* What can we learn from these two verses about Paul's reflections on homosexuality? The following conclusions can be drawn. First, Paul's primary purpose in this entire section is to describe the fall of humanity into the false reality in which it now lives. He wishes to show that this false reality involves one in a false self, which is, although unknown to humanity, God's eschatological judgment for refusal to acknowledge and be obedient to the true God. Both the section on homosexuality and the vice catalog are part of that description. They do not belong in any way to Paul's ethical admonitions, that is, "do this, don't do that."

He does say at the end of the entire section that those who live this way "deserve to die"; doubtless this culpability includes the practice of homosexuality and all of the other sins listed in the vice catalog. Yet one would be hard put to find in the Old Testament specific injunctions against all of the items in the catalog, much less statements of liability to the death penalty for all of them. Thus what Paul probably has in mind, in reference to the death penalty, is the basic sin of the refusal to acknowledge God as God. This is the root of sin and thus is the root of the life that is displeasing to God, which ultimately results in death.

Second, the verses attacking homosexuality seem dependent on Hellenistic Jewish propaganda against Gentiles. While the phrase "males with males" relates to the laws in Leviticus, the likelihood is that Paul is thinking only about pederasty, just as was Philo. There was no other form of male homosexuality in the Greco-Roman world which could come to mind. What may be remarkable is that Paul takes a Hellenistic Jewish attack on paganism and generalizes it to include the entire world, Jew as well as Gentile.

Third, since Paul's intention is theological, not ethical, and since the two verses ultimately stem from his Jewish tradition, it cannot fairly be said that Paul is especially incensed against homosexuality. That he opposes it, on the other hand, is not to be denied.

Finally, does this passage, for all its theological probing, contribute anything new to what might count as a Christian argument against homosexuality? Paul is dependent for his judgment that it

116

is against nature ultimately on Greek, not Jewish sources. There it rests not on some doctrine of creation or philosophical principles, but on what seemingly is thought to count as common-sense observation. I know of no Greco-Roman text which attempts to explain *why* homosexuality is against nature. Paul makes no attempt either.

His insertion of the attack on homosexuality within the theological description of idolatry is directly dependent on Hellenistic Jewish traditions (perhaps specifically the Wisdom of Solomon). But as we have seen, such texts do not explain the relation; it is simply asserted. To this argument Paul adds a middle term. For him idolatry results in a false world with a false self, that is, unnatural. The false self finds homosexuality pleasing and sees nothing wrong in what is for the Apostle a deflection of desire from opposite sex to same sex. Thus for Paul passions directed toward people of the same sex are illustrative of the false self. Paul, no more than the Greeks and Jews, attempted to explain his argument. Perhaps he could not. Perhaps it seemed obvious to him, given his Jewish presuppositions. Thus, or so it seems to me, Paul's theology leaves one in the same ambiguous position that the church finds itself in today. Theological or ethical assertions without adequate rationale are not liable to be convincing except to people already convinced.

At the risk of seeming endlessly repetitive, I close with the observation that Paul thinks of pederasty, and perhaps the more degraded forms of it, when he is attacking homosexuality. Since that is so, then it is not too hard to see how he might have considered it unnatural. Perhaps he was impressed by the lack of mutuality, the physical and emotional humiliation suffered by youths who were forced into slavery or who accepted the degradation of the prostitute. Perhaps it was those particular conditions he had heard of that made him consider homosexuality unnatural, rather than some overarching abstract theological conviction, or even some fiat in his Bible (Paul can easily get out from under biblical fiats when he chooses). Since Paul has not chosen to tell us, we can never find the answers to these wonderments. It is precarious, however, to retreat so entirely into the sanctity of abstract theological/ethical systems that one ignores the actual concrete human situations in which people lived and suffered—and which may have brought the abstract statements into existence in the first place.

1 TIMOTHY 1:9–10

The third and temporally the latest text which is relevant to our discussion is found in 1 Tim. 1:9–10. The passage is similar to 1 Cor. 6:9–10 in that the word *arsenokoitēs* is at issue and the word appears in a catalog of vices. Perhaps because of these similarities, the passage in 1 Timothy is usually given only passing attention. It may prove, however, more interesting and informative than it does at first glimpse.

The author appears to be combating Christian teaching he considers heretical. The people promoting this heresy claim to be, among other things, "teachers of the law." This leads the author to make his own assessment of the place of the law (although it is not clear whether the Mosaic or the civil law is meant). "Now we know that the law is good, if any one uses it lawfully, understanding this, that the law is not laid down for the just but for the lawless . . . " (vv. 8–9a). The word "lawless" then becomes the first vice in a catalog of fourteen items, which can be schematized in the following arrangement:

> lawless, rebellious
> impious, sinner, unholy, profane
> patricide, matricide, murder
> *pornoi, arsenokoitai, andrapodistai*
> liar, perjurer.

Often this list is thought to be ordered according to the Decalogue,[24] but I think the above arrangement does better justice to it. At any rate, contrary to many such lists, this seems to have words grouped together in some recognizable relationships. Lawless and rebellious belong together, perhaps referring to crimes against the civil government. The second line of four items refers to cultic purity, if, as is likely, "sinner" refers to crimes against re-

24. So E. F. Scott, *The Pastoral Epistles* (New York: Harper & Bros., n.d.), p. 10; N. Brox, *Die Pastoralbriefe* (Regensburg: Pustet, 1969), p. 106.

ligious law. The third line of three items collects together various forms of murder. The last line contains two items which point to the telling of falsehoods. The fourth line I have left untranslated, since much depends upon how one interprets these words. The second word, *arsenokoitēs*, is of course familiar to us by now. But what are the meanings of the other two?

Pornos. This word in normal Greek usage means "male prostitute" and appears several times in the literature we have analyzed, pointing to either the male who sells himself, or the slave in the brothel house.[25] Hellenistic Jewish and early Christian usage, however, skews the apparently straightforward definition. The word, not surprisingly, does not appear in any Septuagint book except the post-Old Testament *Sirach* 23:16–18. It does appear a few times in the New Testament. The problem here is that the word in *Sirach* and in the New Testament seems to have a meaning broader than "male prostitute" and is usually taken by scholars to refer to sexual crimes in general.[26] This is not the place to address the general usage in the New Testament and *Sirach*, although I suspect our lack of knowledge and awareness of the prominence of the male prostitute in Greco-Roman society may have misled us often into ignoring the possibility, at least, that sometimes even in the biblical writings *pornos* may retain its usual meaning.

However that may be, surely the context, insofar as it can be derived, must determine the meaning in any particular place. There is no a priori reason why *pornos* in 1 Timothy could not refer to the male prostitute. There is, it is admitted, very little context in a catalog. The juxtaposition of *pornos* with *arsenokoitēs*, however, should give us pause before we translate the word in a more gen-

---

25. E.g., Demosthenes, *Against Androtion* 73; idem, *Epistle* 4. 10f; Aristophanes, *Plutus*, lines 153–57; Xenophon, *Memorabilia* I. vi. 13; Aeschines, *Timarchus* 52, 119, 137 (these, however, in adjectival or verbal forms).

26. For example, Walter Bauer (W. F. Arndt and F. W. Gingrich), while noting that in classical literature it can mean "male prostitute," says that "in our lit. quite gener. *fornicator, one who practices sexual immorality*" [italics theirs], *A Greek-English Lexicon of the New Testament* (Chicago and London: Univ. of Chicago Press, 1957), p. 700. The word does not occur frequently (nine times in the New Testament), the majority of times in vice catalogs. It is, interestingly, the word which appears in all three of the catalogs in 1 Corinthins 5 and 6, which I translated "immoral." I do not think one can in those cases press for a narrow meaning of the term.

eral fashion. There is no reason why the same relationship that we saw existing between *malakos* and *arsenokoitēs*, that is, between the youth who is used and the adult who uses him, could not also pertain to the two words in 1 Timothy. *Pornos* could effectively function in relation to *arsenokoitēs* in precisely the same way as *malakos* does in 1 Corinthians.

This possibility is further supported by the third word: *andropodistes* (only here in the New Testament). This word means "kidnapper" or "slave dealer." While in our culture these definitions carry differences of meaning, in the culture of the first century C.E. they would be synonymous. A person is kidnapped normally only to be sold into slavery.[27] One reason a handsome boy or beautiful girl would be kidnapped is to provide slaves for brothel houses. Thus the kidnapper or slave dealer is in part one who is involved in the sexual profession, with being ultimately responsible for the *pornos*, who is used by *arsenokoitēs*.[28]

The three words would thus fit together and could be translated: "male prostitutes, males who lie [with them], and slave-dealers [who procure them]." This makes coherent sense of the three successive words and should, I believe, be considered a serious possibility. One could then consider whether the author of 1 Timothy intended his earlier reference to the law to refer to biblical injunctions or civil law. I do not think the question can be finally answered. If, however, he were reflecting on the Septuagint version of the Old Testament, then he would have found there an injunction against the *arsenokoitēs* (Leviticus 18 and 20), the *pornos* (Deut. 23:18), and the kidnapper (Exod. 4:16; Deut. 24:7). Since I have already suggested that *arsenokoitēs* must be a Hellenistic Jewish coinage, and since the vice list here does not seem dependent on that in 1 Cor. 6:9–10, it may indeed be likely that this list originated in Hellenistic Jewish circles.

I thus draw the conclusion that the vice list in 1 Timothy is not condemnatory of homosexuality in general, not even pederasty in general, but that specific form of pederasty which consisted of the

27. Cf. Philo, *Special Laws* IV. 13f.
28. Should "kidnapper" not be related to the preceding words in some fashion, it would be unique in this list, since all the other words have some connection with a previous or following word.

enslaving of boys or youths for sexual purposes, and the use of these boys by adult males. Perhaps the effeminate call-boy is also included in the condemnation, but I see no way of making a judgment on the matter.

CONCLUSIONS

1. The New Testament church was not very much concerned about homosexuality as a problem, at least to judge from the evidence of the texts. All three instances referring to homosexuality are directly or indirectly from preformed traditions, either Greek or Jewish. No single New Testament author considers the issue important enough to write his own sentence about it! The language comes entirely from already established conventions in both Greek and Jewish cultures. The argument from nature is the most common form of attack on pederasty in Greco-Roman texts. Shamefulness is a common word in the same literature. The phrase "male with male" stems directly from biblical law, and the word *arsenokoitēs*, so foreign to the Greek terminology, is a coinage made in Hellenistic Judaism. Even in Romans 1, where Paul integrates the illustration of homosexuality into his larger theological argument, there is no significant advance over the already established linkage in Hellenistic Judaism between idolatry and pagan vices, including pederasty.

2. Female homosexuality gets even less attention than male, appearing only in Romans 1, and here with less emphasis, it would seem, than male homosexuality. This is doubtlessly because little was said in the Greco-Roman world about lesbianism, and because in biblical law no penalties attached to such female practices.

3. The two vice lists attack very specific forms of pederasty, forms which were opposed by serious minded pagan authors: the adult use of male prostitutes, especially the borderline instances of effeminate free males who let themselves be used sexually. Pederasty in general, much less homosexuality in general, is not included in these indictments.

4. Only in Romans 1 is there a negative judgment made on both female as well as male homosexuality which could be considered a general indictment. Even here, the entire cumulative evidence we

have looked at throughout this book suggests that despite the general language Paul, with regard to the statement about male homosexuality, must have had, *could only have had*, pederasty in mind. That Paul uses here the argument from nature might mean, of course, that he would have made the same judgment about *any* form of homosexuality. No one can legitimately conclude, however, that he would have done so. We just do not know. What he would have said about the contemporary model of adult/adult mutuality in same-sex relationships, we shall also never know. I am not sure it is even useful to speculate.

5. Thus the ultimate issue to be raised from our journey through this particular cultural and religious history is the legitimacy of using New Testament judgments about a particular form and model of homosexuality to inform decisions about the acceptability of a contemporary form of homosexuality, which projects an entirely different model. Since the models are so different, some would say mutually exclusive, it cannot be a foregone conclusion that the New Testament can be helpfully used in today's discussion *without seriously violating the integrity of the New Testament itself*. To what extent is it legitimate canonically, theologically, ethically, and historically to use the judgments of the New Testament to decide, or even inform, current denominational debates? To this question I turn in the concluding chapter.

8
Taking a Stand

We are now through with our detailed study of the past. What, if anything, does this say to our present? That is, does what we have learned help us in our reflections on, and decision-making about, the place of gay Christians in the church? How may this book help us to take a stand, as take a stand we must surely do, in the future, if not at the moment? This issue has created so much heat and is, indeed, so complex that it is obvious no single stand will be agreed upon by all. There is no one view that will win consensus, whatever the outcome of voting in church assemblies. When I undertake in these remaining pages to offer my own evaluation of the uses and abuses of the Bible, I can only do it knowing that what for some people is a legitimate use, for others is an abuse, and vice versa. I am called upon, however, to make that evaluation which seems to me to be true to the witness of Scripture and which makes an honest assessment of how those writings should or should not be used in today's debate.

Quite clearly the previous chapters indicated that I cannot in conscience accept the view that makes biblical injunctions into necessarily eternal ethical truths, independent of the historical and cultural context. The meaning of the statements for me is first the meaning they *had* for the writers in their own, concrete situation. The possibility that they may *have* meaning for today depends on whether two additional conditions are met: (1) The biblical statements must be consonant with the larger, major theological and ethical judgments which lie at the heart not only of Scripture but of the historical church throughout the ages. (2) The context today must bear a reasonable similarity to the context of the statements at the time of writing.

123

In chapter 1 we surveyed how some authors brought the large theological motifs prominent in the Bible to bear on the issue of homosexuality.[1] Such themes as creation, sin, judgment, grace, love, care for the neighbor, and the upbuilding of the community certainly touch in one way or another virtually every ethical issue imaginable, including homosexuality. While I think that such an approach is necessary, it is also extremely complex. All but the most conservative believers will acknowledge that the Bible is not completely unified in its thoughts, that there are, in fact, contradictions about what is true and right within its pages. On the one hand this makes it uncertain that there is a single teaching about creation, or a unified notion of the meaning of sin, etc. On the other, it does allow some space for a search for a center, for the Gospel (as Luther maintained) which might overrule some specific sections of Scripture not seen to be consonant with such a center. And this in turn means that it is conceivable that specific injunctions of the Bible may be disallowed because they do not meet the essential core of the Gospel. At any rate, this use of Scripture to inform contemporary decision-making about homosexuality can cut both ways, can be used by both proponents and opponents, using even the same motifs! That theological task, however necessary, is so different from the attempt to recover social backgrounds, the theme of this volume, that I cannot speak to it in these pages.

I thus limit myself to an assessment of the contemporary relevance of the specific injunctions against homosexuality we have inspected. But this means, for purposes of discussion within Christian circles, that our primary focus must be on the statements in the New Testament rather than the Old. This is true because Christian hermeneutics, both in practice and in theory, concedes the priority of the New Testament over the Old. The new dispensation has brought to an end certain dimensions of the old.

The number of Old Testament laws the church has discarded is immense. We commonly—and anachronistically—think we make distinctions only between the moral laws and the cultic and purity laws. Not only is this a false dichotomy to apply to Israelite law, not only is it not a distinction the New Testament makes in any formal fashion, it also is not our own principle of selection, at least

1. Cf. above, pp. 9f.

not our only one. For example, in Lev. 19:9 there is an injunction not to reap one's field to the border, so that the poor may have that produce. In Lev. 19:13 there is also a law which prescribes that a hired laborer should be paid daily. These are obviously ethical laws, but which no Christian, to my knowledge, feels it his duty to keep today. Examples could be multiplied and the list expanded to include theological estimations of the nature of God and what He wills for humankind. The conclusion, thus, that Christian assessment about homosexuality and God's will should depend primarily upon New Testament rather than Old Testament texts seems justified.

At this point in our thinking, the second condition mentioned above emerges as absolutely essential: *The context today must bear a reasonable similarity to the context which called the biblical statements into existence.* Given the above, this means that only if the context which led to the creation of New Testament judgments against homosexuality is similar to the context of the gay movement within Christianity today, can biblical injunctions be relevant in contemporary denominational discussions.

This conclusion should be accepted, I would maintain, no matter whether one is "conservative" or "liberal" in views of the Bible. *Even if* a biblical injunction is taken as an eternally valid rule for Christian living, one must first determine *what* it proposes or prohibits. Only exegesis, not hermeneutics, can decide what the eternally valid rule is about. Deut. 23:17–18 is an example. It may still be seen as a rule applicable for today, but if exegesis demonstrates that it does not pertain to homosexuality, then it immediately becomes irrelevant for our purposes.

Paul's judgments may thus be eternally valid but can, nevertheless, be *valid only against what he opposed.* If he opposed something specific, then his statements cannot be generalized beyond the limitations of his intentionality without violating the integrity of the Scripture. Thus New Testament statements can be applied only to situations which are similar to those addressed by the New Testament.[2]

It is equally legitimate, however, to turn the argument around.

2. For an instructive application of this approach to the issue of the pacifism of Jesus, cf. Martin Hengel, *Victory over Violence* (Philadelphia: Fortress Press, 1973), especially my introductory comments, pp. xxi–xxii.

If the contemporary situation is *not* reasonably similar, then biblical injunctions cannot become answers to contemporary questions. If the situation proves to be noticeably different, then it is the proper course of action not to use such injunctions to decide contemporary issues, *however much the believer considers the Bible to be authoritative.*

The brunt of my exegesis in the previous chapters has been to show that in the Greco-Roman world there was one basic model of male homosexuality. (I had to conclude that our sources did not permit us to make any certain statements about female homosexuality.) While I tried not to minimize exceptions or partial deviations from the model of pederasty, I thought it fair to conclude that the majority of such relationships were, both by definition and practice, characterized by lack of mutuality, both spiritually and physically. The more one shifts attention to the call-boy and outright prostitution, which 1 Cor. 6:9–10 and 1 Tim. 1:9 attack, the more the practices opposed are those abusive of human rights and dignity. *Thus what the New Testament was against was the image of homosexuality as pederasty and primarily here its more sordid and dehumanizing dimensions.* One would regret it if somebody in the New Testament had not opposed such dehumanization.

If this is so, the necessary criterion of reasonable similarity between the New Testament period and today's model of homosexual relationships does not obtain. The ideal, at least, of adult homosexuality today, certainly within Christian groups, is that of a caring and mutual relationship between consenting adults. That this model is not simply an idealization is indicated by the study of A. Bell and M. Weinberg; I think it important to quote at length from one of their conclusions.

> Finally, our data tend to belie the notion that homosexual affairs are apt to be inferior imitations of heterosexuals' premarital or marital involvements. The fact that homosexual liaisons, unlike those of their heterosexual counterparts, are not encouraged or legally sanctioned by the society probably accounts for their relative instability. But the stability of a relationship may not be the only or even the chief criterion for judging its quality. Our data indicate that a relatively steady relationship with a love partner is a very meaningful event in the life of a homosexual man or woman. From our respondents' descriptions, these affairs are apt to involve an emotional ex-

change and commitment similar to the kinds that heterosexuals experience, and most of the homosexual respondents thought that they and their partners had benefited personally from their involvement and were at least somewhat unhappy when it was over. The fact that they generally went on to a subsequent affair with another partner seems to suggest a parallel with heterosexuals' remarriage after divorce rather than any particular emotional immaturity or maladjustment. In any case, most of our homosexual respondents spoke of these special relationships in positive terms and clearly were not content to limit their sexual contacts to impersonal sex.[3]

I do not, and could not even if I did, wish to deny the reality of dehumanizing patterns in homosexual activity today, any more than I would deny they also exist within heterosexual patterns. I am certainly aware that it is precarious to compare the best of one culture with the worst of another. There is casual sex between homosexuals today, just as among heterosexuals. One hears of youthful male prostitutes, as well as female. The temptation must exist for some males today to assume the role of the call-boy, pretty much as it existed in ancient culture. I would hope that the church would fight as hard as possible against these as well as all other forms of dehumanization.

The *fact* remains, however, that the basic model in today's Christian homosexual community is so different from the model attacked by the New Testament that the criterion of reasonable similarity of context is not met. The conclusion I have to draw seems inevitable: *Biblical judgments against homosexuality are not relevant to today's debate.* They should no longer be used in denominational discussions about homosexuality, should in no way be a weapon to justify refusal of ordination, *not because the Bible is not authoritative,* but simply because it does not address the issues involved.

Argument will fairly be made against this judgment from Romans 1. There two things are evident. The first is that Paul makes no age distinctions. The second is that both male and female homosexuality are attacked as being contrary to nature. The first observation has already been answered. It is typical of Jewish statements to make no age differentials, even when the author clearly

---

3. A. Bell and M. Weinberg, *Homosexualities: A Study of Diversity among Men and Women* (New York: Simon and Schuster, 1978), p. 102.

has pederasty in mind.⁴ Just so, Paul, I have argued, has to be thinking about pederasty.

The second observation is more difficult to answer and the response more subtle. I have shown that the charge that pederasty is contrary to nature is the most commonplace of Greco-Roman objections to such relationships. Paul is simply repeating what he must have heard on street corners over and over again. It is extremely unlikely that he has any reference here to some "biblical doctrine of creation." This does not mean his judgment is to be ignored. Paul *does* say pederasty is contrary to nature. As already said, given the nonmutual and frequently dehumanizing qualities of such relationships in Paul's day, that is not surprising and is indeed to be applauded as a general statement, from which there might well be actual exceptions.

The question remains: would Paul have said the same thing about the current model of the caring adult relationship of mutuality? I have no way of knowing. Let no one think that I am trying to turn Paul into an advocate of contemporary homosexuality. He might still be opposed. *The point is that there is no way of knowing.* One could argue that since Paul says homosexuality is against nature, he is thinking specifically of the "unnatural" use of the sexual organs and would thus be opposed to such "unnaturalness" no matter what the age or mutuality of the partners were.

On the other hand, no one can deny that all of us are influenced substantially by the reality we see around us, or think we see, or hear talked about. No doubt Paul knew about slave brothels; no doubt he must have heard of, maybe frequently passed in the streets, effeminate call-boys. At least according to Philo they were very obvious in public places.⁵ If pederasty in its actuality was so prone to nonmutual and dehumanizing dimensions, and if this is what Paul mostly knew of, or had heard about, then it is hardly surprising that he would be opposed to it as an institution and that he would have picked up the most commonplace of objections to it.

Suppose, however, that what he knew was an entirely different model. If he had known at firsthand caring adult homosexual re-

4. Cf. the discussion of Philo, pp. 88f., 91 above.
5. Philo, *Special Laws* III. 37–39.

lationships, if he had had respected and talented homosexual friends within the church and its leadership, what would he have said? I do not know and I do not think anyone can presume to know. It cannot be simply concluded that he would have attacked it with the same terms.

It may seem surprising to read an author who has spent his entire adult life studying the Bible argue that the Scriptures are irrelevant and provide no help in the heated debate today. *I regard this to be true about the specific passages we have analyzed.* Yet the Bible with its great thematics of our faith must still be heard and will still provide guidance. The search for the basic truths of the Bible, along with a serious grappling with psychological and sociological resources, should now become the primary aid in helping us reach decisions.

Of course this means we have no longer any simple way of deciding the issue. Once the biblical injunctions are eliminated from the discussion, once the Bible ceases to be used as a bludgeon for whatever side, then all of us are thrown into a situation where none of us are knowers but all only seekers. This is in itself consonant with the human reality revealed in the New Testament, in which we walk by faith not sight, and where we know at best only partially. Given this situation there is no room for arrogance, for overconfidence, for a prideful mind which refuses to listen to others.

As we face the challenge of the difficult decisions that lie ahead, we may no longer use the Bible as a simplistic weapon. But it does not leave us comfortless. My prayer is that we may all remember and reremember what Paul implies in 1 Cor. 13:12, that it is more important to be aware that we are graced by God than it is to be sure we know all the answers. May that be the unifying ground of our reconciliation with each other and the basis of our ongoing search for wisdom.

APPENDIX A

On the Question of
Nonpederastic
Male Homosexuality

Much of my argument depends upon the judgment frequently stated above, that the *only* model of male homosexuality was pederasty, and that even deviations in the usual age patterns of pederasty did not disturb the functioning of the model itself. Thus this conclusion is a particularly sensitive issue. Have I fairly presented all the evidence, or have I missed some that could call my conclusion into question?

On the one hand I do not pretend to have exhausted all the material. Even if I knew all of it, I could not present it in such a volume as this. On the other, I do think I have presented enough to demonstrate amply that the pederastic model was at the very least the dominant and always assumed pattern for male homosexual relationships. In this Appendix, however, I want to collect data which might, to some people, suggest that a nonpederastic model existed alongside of the pederastic. Much, but not all, of the material has been previously discussed.

GENERAL SLOGANS

Paul, as we have seen, speaks in the most general terms in Rom. 1:26–27, writing about "males committing shameless acts with males" (au. trans.). Nothing in the language itself would force one to limit his meaning to pederasty. We have also seen that Philo writes equally generally of "males for males," even though the context of the passage clearly shows he is thinking of pederasty.[1] I argued that in both of these instances, the language of these

1. Philo, *Contemplative Life* 59–62.

Jewish authors was probably influenced by the laws in Leviticus. There are, however, similar slogans occasionally in the Greek literature as well, literature that could not be influenced by the Septuagint. Does this data suggest Greek authors knew of a non-pederastic male homosexuality? I will cite three examples.

> When male (*arsen*) unites with female (*thelus*) for procreation, the pleasure experienced is held to be due to nature, but contrary to nature when male mates with male or female with female (Plato, *Laws* I. 636C²).

> Whence until now the desires of animals have involved intercourse neither of male [*arsen*] with male nor of female [*thelus*] with female. But [there are] many such among your noble and good [classes] (Plutarch, *Beasts are rational* 990D).

> Do not transgress the beds of nature for unlawful passion. Male [*arsen*] beds do not please even the beasts. Nor shall females [here a derivative from *thelus* is used] imitate the beds of males (Pseudo-Phocylides, *Maxims*, lines 190–92).

These statements have in common with Paul several features. (*a*) They are general, nonspecific judgments. (*b*) They use the terms for male and female which are not age-differentiated. (*c*) They all make negative judgments on homosexuality. To this should be added that Plato explicitly and Plutarch implicitly share with Paul the argument from nature. Seen in this regard, Rom. 1:26–27 could be seen as a commonplace of Greek moral wisdom.

The question for us, however, is not now the source of these slogan-type statements but whether in their generality they point to male homosexual practices that are outside the limits of pederasty, for example, whether there were same-age reciprocal relationships between males? To answer the question, at least for the authors of these slogans, we must determine, if possible, what they understood to be included under the broad categories of male and female. Is it possible from the context of the author's writings to interpret the slogans? That is, do the writers in effect tell us elsewhere what they mean by the slogans? Fortunately, it is possible to answer affirmatively in all three instances.

From all the evidence already presented about Plato, it is obvi-

2. The translation of Plato is that of R. G. Bury, *Laws*, LCL (Cambridge, Mass.: Harvard Univ. Press, 1961).

ous that for him male homosexuality is equitable with pederasty, however much he is acquainted with adults who remain in the passive relationship with older men. But we are not left to the other treatises. In the *Laws* itself, when Plato begins to discuss specifically the issue of homosexuality, he does it in the terms with which we have become familiar: pederasty, lover and beloved, problems in the gymnasia, and of the need for nonsexual pederasty to be the norm in his ideal state.[3] He is strangely silent about female homosexuality.

With regard to Plutarch, the matter is equally clear from the *Erōtikos*. There, as we have seen, the argument between homosexuality and heterosexuality is argued exclusively on the models of pederasty and marriage. In *Whether Beasts are Rational*, it is instructive to look at the examples the pig (who verbalizes the slogan) gives of homosexuality. There are three: (*a*) Agamemnon pursuing Argynnus (according to one authority, a pederastic situation);[4] (*b*) Heracles pursuing a beardless youth; (*c*) a soldier putting up a graffiti, "fair is Achilles," a slogan used to refer to an *erōmenos*. That the pig finds this ascription directed to an adult warrior strange or even offensive is signaled by his remark that Achilles at this time was already the father of a son.[5] Thus it seems clear that Plutarch assumes "normal" homosexual relationships are pederastic, since the example of the soldier and Achilles is seen as abhorrent. This author is also virtually silent about female homosexuality.

Pseudo-Phocylides is more difficult to interpret because we do not have other treatises by this same author. Nevertheless, the *Maxims* itself offers some help. At the very end the author declares that boys should not have long, coiffured hair, that the youthful period of a beautiful boy (*pais*) should be guarded carefully, "for many are maddened by desire for male intercourse."[6] This last citation is particularly important, since, while the author here uses the general word for male, he is obviously thinking about the seduction of boys. That is, he can use the general term

3. Plato, *Laws* VIII. 836C–837D.
4. M. H. E. Meier, enlarged by L. R. de Pogey-Castries, *Histoire de l'amour grec dans l'antiquite* (Paris: Stendahl et Compagnie, 1930) p. 39.
5. Plutarch, *Whether Beasts are Rational* 990DE.
6. Pseudo-Phocylides, *Maxims*, lines 210–14.

precisely because nobody is going to mistake his meaning. Thus the conclusion, unless other evidence could be brought to bear, is that in his general slogan he must also be pointing at pederasty.[7] He gives no hint as to what he had in mind about female homosexuality.

I cannot, of course, *prove* that the male half of these slogans refers to pederasty; proof is beyond possibility. Nevertheless, I do think it precarious to use the slogans to claim that a broader set of practices other than pederasty is intended by the authors, unless further evidence can be found that *specifically* reveals a model or models other than the one that was so common in the world of this time. What the female part of the slogan may have included is beyond recovery. It is even possible that it functions more to balance the rhetoric than to indicate some specific content.

HOMOSEXUALITY BETWEEN YOUTHS OF APPROXIMATELY THE SAME AGE

If there is any evidence which points to same-age homosexuality, it is between youths (meirakioi). Some evidence for youths engaging in sexual activity with each other comes from the vases pictured and described in K. J. Dover.[8] As already suggested, these paintings were made mostly between 570 and 470 B.C.E. and thus can speak only for a comparatively early time. Nevertheless, it is clear from these that youths were attracted to the beauty of other youths (the youth is defined in the vase paintings as one who does not yet have a beard) and indulged in sexual encounters, including anal intercourse, among themselves. To what extent these paintings suggest actual and lasting friendships between such youths is impossible to determine.

Scattered throughout the relevant literature are a few instances of more or less same-age youths having relationships with each other. Xenophon makes a passing reference to the relationship that Menon of Thessaly had, while a youth, with a barbarian

7. Cf. also Athenaeus, *Deipnosophists* XII. 540E. Here a tyrant, Polycrates, is shown to be a pederast, but the language speaks of his desire for intercourse with "males."

8. Cf. his plates, R 27, 59, 196, 223, 243, 547, 637, 851, 954, in K. J. Dover, *Greek Homosexuality* (Cambridge, Mass: Harvard Univ. Press, 1978).

named Ariaeus. Ariaeus liked youths (*meirakios*) and was already bearded. Yet the beardless Menon is said to have had Ariaeus as his favorite (*paidika*).[9] Thus Menon is the *erastēs*; the older Ariaeus, the *erōmenos*. The two were probably not significantly different in age, since the greater the age differential was, the harder it is to understand Menon taking the active role.

A more detailed description is given by the same author in his *Symposium*. At the banquet are two youths in love, Critobulus and Cleinias. Judging from the banter, it is Critobulus who is the active partner, who considers Cleinias to be beautiful and who, presumably, actually kisses him during the course of the discussion. Socrates comments: "This hot flame of his [Critobulus's] was kindled in the days when they used to go to school together."[10] Thus pictured here is a passionate relationship between two youths of roughly the same age.

Further evidence may be found in Achilles Tatius. The pederast Clinias is described as *neos* (another term for boy or youth) and his love is labeled *meirakion*. There must be some age differential assumed, but it is not necessarily much, since the father of the *meirakion* is ready to marry him to a woman.[11] Later in the same romance another young man (*neaniskos*) is encountered by the hero. He also is a pederast and loves a *meirakion*.[12] Again there is some age differential stated, but it is not likely great.

Perhaps the most famous example, however, comes from the biting pen of Cicero in his attack on Mark Anthony.[13] The orator accuses Anthony of being a common prostitute (*vulgare scortum*) as a boy. He points to a time when Anthony was taken into the house of one Curio and kept for sexual purposes. Cicero suggests Anthony was playing the passive role, as if he were then a wife. Curio, however, was not an adult, because he was still living with his father. The Curio in question was born about 84 B.C.E.; Anthony, about 82. Thus they were roughly the same age.

These passages thus suggest that, occasionally, essentially same-

9. Xenophon, *Anabasis* II. vi. 28.
10. Xenophon, *Symposium* IV. 23, vol. IV, LCL.
11. Achilles Tatius, *Leucippe and Clitophon* I. 7.
12. Ibid., II. 33–34.
13. Cicero, *Philippics* II. 44f.

age youths had passions for each other. But three reservations need to be stated. *First*, this seems from the evidence to be an infrequently realized pattern, perhaps most prevalent just when one of the youths was becoming an adult and experimenting with the change from the role of the *erōmenos* to that of the *erastēs*. Thus, it marks the moment of transition. *Second*, I know of no similar reports or stories about adult-adult relationships, beyond those pertaining to men who prolonged their passive role and youthful desirability into a time when others had long since exchanged the passive role for the active. The desired sexual object was and always remained the beautiful youth, most like in appearance to a woman. An adult who sought after another adult his own age would probably have been laughed at. *Three*, even when same-age youths were in relation with each other, the texts clearly point to one as the active, the other as the passive. Thus the pederastic model of inequality remains functional even in these cases.

ADULT ERŌMENOI

In rare instances, texts suggest a second bending of the normal pederastic pattern. This occurred when the youth prolonged his passive role beyond the time when normally he would have exchanged it for the active. We have already studied the evidence for systematic removal of hair to produce smooth skins and beardless faces, the adoption of coiffured hair, perfume, and even women's clothing, and the use of castration on slaves. The older the person attempting, or having to maintain his passive status, the more the person seems to have made use of specific women's attire and habits. The texts suggest that there were three reasons why an adult male would be found in this category.

1. He chose this life style because it was personally pleasing. Some men seem to have positively desired, for whatever psychological reasons, to remain in this subordinate relationship with other men. When we have a text, however, that is explicit enough to name the people involved, the *erastēs* is still usually older than the adult *erōmenos*. Perhaps the most famous example, as we have seen, is the beautiful Agathon. According to Plato Pausanias be-

The New Testament and Homosexuality

came the *erastēs* of Agathon when the youth was eighteen, and the relation lasted for several years.[14] The date of the dinner narrated by Plato in the *Symposium* is 416 B.C.E. Agathon, born about 447, would then have been 31. Thus at this age he is represented as remaining an *erōmenos*, still called a *neaniskos* in the dialogue, doubtlessly because of his continued youthful beauty.[15] He is portrayed as being attracted to Socrates, who was about twenty years his senior. As we have seen, Aristophanes turns Agathon into an effeminate, adopting women's clothes and customs. On Aristophanes' treatment of Agathon, Dover's comment is worth consideration. "His [Agathon's] unwillingness to grow out of the *erōmenos* state into sexual dominance will have been sufficient reason for Aristophanes to treat him as 'fucked'; whether he declined an active heterosexual role, and whether he wore feminine clothing, we do not know."[16]

2. He chose this life style because it was lucrative. Here the callboy emerges. If the person found the *erōmenos* life a profitable one, he might be tempted to parlay his beauty into profit even in his adult life. The most vivid and sad picture of such a person is drawn by Juvenal.[17] Here we meet an old man, Naevolus, who has earned his living by prostituting himself to both women and men (and perhaps as the active partner). Now that he is old, how-

---

14. For this cf. Dover, *Greek Homosexuality*, p. 84. This depends upon the accuracy of the implication in Plato's *Symposium* that the relationship is still in existence at the time set for the dinner, cf. *Symposium* 193BC.

15. Plato, *Symposium* 198A.

16. Dover, *Greek Homosexuality*, p. 144. A second such prolongation might possibly be seen in the relationship between Alcibiades and Socrates. The brash and dissolute youth confesses to have been in love with Socrates (who is about twenty years older than Alcibiades), and at the occasion of the Symposium would have been about thirty-four years old. The passion which Alcibiades admits he has had for Socrates and the attempt at seduction is, however, represented as a past event. He also calls himself, in relation to Socrates, *paidika*, a term which ordinarily is reserved for actual youths (217B). Although the youthful Alcibiades is represented as taking the initiative, this functions in the dialogue to highlight the steadfast refusal of Socrates to stoop to sexual encounters with his beloveds. Thus there is little comparison that can be made between Agathon and Alcibiades.

Demosthenes (*Epistle* 4) attacks the adult Thesamenes with accusations of homosexual relations with a male prostitute. This is noteworthy only because in this instance Thesamenes plays the effeminate, passive role—he suffers as a woman (*paschei d'hōs gunē*), while the male prostitute performs the active role, another example of a person continuing the *erōmenos* role into adulthood. Again it is important to note that even here the pederastic model is not jettisoned but continued.

17. Juvenal, *Satire* IX.

136

ever, his client does not want him anymore; he has turned to fairer and doubtlessly more youthful males. Juvenal may have exaggerated this picture, but it most likely mirrors to a certain extent actual human situations he knew.

A second, but more doubtful example may be seen in the person of Timarchus, so successfully vilified by Aeschines. As we have seen, Timarchus was a notorious call-boy. The question is whether there is evidence he plied his trade beyond the normal period of his youthful attractiveness. This seems doubtful, for Aeschines does not mention it. The orator begins his attack by saying that he will not mention the sins of Timarchus committed when the latter was a boy (*pais*), but will take up the story when he has become a youth (*meirakion*).[18] All of the events which involved the accused in prostitution are spoken of as if they are in the past tense. Had Timarchus continued to the present to indulge in such activities, it is incredible that Aeschines would not have mentioned them. Thus Timarchus probably cannot be counted among those who prolonged their *erōmenos* into adulthood, even if he did use himself in this manner as an older youth.

Perhaps better evidence can be found in a speech of Demosthenes. Here the orator accuses one Androtion of prostitution, in much the same fashion as Timarchus was accused by Aeschines.[19] The accused is also an adult, since he is speaking in assembly and proposing laws. The text seems to suggest that at the time of the speech Androtion is still prostituting himself, although the issue perhaps ought to be left in doubt.

3. He is a slave and has no choice. The celebrated case of Nero's slave, Sporus, immediately comes to mind. Nero has Sporus castrated, given a woman's name, and dressed in women's clothes, so that he can actually become the "wife" of the emperor.[20] Dio ascribes practices of castration followed by female dressing of boys to the Persians and refers elsewhere more generally to men who emasculate boys.[21] In both instances these must be slaves. Lucian refers in passing to an adult slave, who has performed, although

18. Aeschines, *Timarchus* 39.
19. Demosthenes, *Speeches* 22.
20. Dio Chrysostom 21. 6–8; Suetonius, *Nero* 28.
21. Dio Chrysostom 21. 4 and 77/8. 36.

now too old for it to be seemly, sexual services for his master, still with shaven chin.[22] Seneca suggests the Romans also did similar things to their slaves. He describes slaves' duties at a banquet. One is a wine-server, who is kept beardless by hair removal, is dressed in women's clothes, and divides "his time between his master's drunkenness and his lust (*libidinem*)." "In the chamber he must be a man, at the feast a boy" (*in cubicula vir, in convivio puer*).[23]

CONCLUSION

It is now time to collect the evidence and assess it. The question for us is whether any of this material suggests a basically different pattern or a real alternative to pederasty. I do not think that it does.

The general references to homosexual activity by males and females cannot be used to justify a different pattern *unless specific examples of different patterns are available for inspection.* To the best of my knowledge, there are no other such patterns. Thus the context of the treatises and the culture as a whole makes it clear that the pattern that is in the mind of the authors of the slogans is precisely that of pederasty, not of some other sort.

The instances of an adult accepting the *erōmenos* life style seem rare and are looked upon with disdain by authors, even those who accept other forms of pederasty. Furthermore, the pattern of pederasty, with all its attendant inequalities, is not left behind but is continued. The adult *erōmenos* accepts the same relationship with the *erastēs* as he did when he was a *pais* or *meirakion*. It surely counts as an example of stunted emotional growth. The saddest cases are those of the slaves, who had no choice but to accept the degradation and humiliation inevitable in such forced servitude.

Only in the case of relationships between same-age youths can there be any thought of an alternative model. Yet even here the facts that the active-passive roles were adopted and the likelihood that the youth taking the active role is in the transitional period from youth to active adult make it improbable that a really differ-

22. Lucian, *Timon* 22.
23. Seneca, *Epistle* XLVII. 7.

ent model is in play. Even if it were different, it does not seem, to judge from the evidence, to have been very prominent.

I do not wish to use Procrustes' bed to force all male homosexual activities in the Greco-Roman world to a simple form of pederasty. Obviously there were many different avenues pederasty could and did take, and, no doubt, many subtle nuances in concrete cases that would never be reflected in our texts. Nor do I wish the syllogism to seem to be: All homosexuality was pederastic; all pederasty was constitutive of inequality and thus evil; therefore all homosexuality was evil. I do not doubt that friendships of good passion and tender caring existed. I *am* suggesting that if we interpret pederasty supplely enough to include the continuation of that model into these borderline cases, then it is certain that pederasty was the only *model* in existence in the world of this time. That proposed by twentieth-century gay liberation movements was, without question, entirely absent.

APPENDIX B

Female Homosexuality in the Greco-Roman World

One of the most surprising things a researcher in this area learns is that there is virtually nothing in the texts about female homosexuality. A student limiting his or her study to biblical and Jewish traditions should perhaps expect that this would be the case, since the Old Testament says nothing about it and only in the "slogan" of Paul in Rom. 1:26 does the New Testament refer to it. Nevertheless it is startling that, in comparison with the many references we have discussed about pederasty, so few examples or references to female homosexuality are available in the Greco-Roman literature. The frustration of the person interested in the subject is well expressed by K. J. Dover: "That female homosexuality and the attitude of women to male homosexuality can both be discussed within one part of one chapter reflects the paucity of women writers and artists in the Greek world and the virtual silence of male writers and artists on these topics."[1] Either the male author had no interest in such relationships or no knowledge about it, or, as Dover seems to suggest, he avoided it because it was a threat to the male ego.[2] How could women like women more than they liked men?

Since the evidence is sparse, discussion often centers on questions about Sappho of Lesbos and the community of women, or school of girls, she founded (if she founded anything). Whether

---

1. K. J. Dover, *Greek Homosexuality* (Cambridge, Mass: Harvard Univ. Press, 1978), p. 171; cf. also John Boswell, *Christianity, Social Tolerance, and Homosexuality* (Chicago: Univ. of Chicago Press, 1980), pp. 82f.

2. At least he "suggests the possibility that the complete silence of comedy on the subject of female homosexuality is a reflex of male anxiety" (*Greek Homosexuality*, pp. 172f).

140

Sappho actually was a homosexual and whether sexual acts were involved, if she was, apparently cannot be answered with any assurance. The poetic fragments are not sufficient to enable conclusive judgment. For our purposes the discussion is not very important, since whether a woman in the sixth century B.C.E. was or was not homosexual helps us very little in establishing what might be the reality during the time of Paul. There have been recent discussions of the problems about Sappho which relieve us here from reviewing the pros and cons.[3]

The real task is to discover what evidence there is for a later period. I lean on the competent authority of Dover for the classical period. "Classical Attic literature refers once, and once only, to female homosexuality."[4] He is referring to the speech of Aristophanes in Plato's *Symposium*. One kind of originally whole person was that composed of all female parts. "All the women who are sections of the woman have no great fancy for men: they are inclined rather to women, and of this stock are the she-minions."[5] The word euphemistically translated "she-minions" is *hetairistria*, which refers to women who use nonmale means to reach sexual orgasm (for instance, artificial phalli, called by the ancients *olisboi*). There are vase paintings showing women using such devices, although these could as easily be heterosexually inclined women as women using them in the context of homosexual encounters.[6] That we know of double *olisboi*, that is, those that could be used by two women at the same time facing each other, suggests that the *olisboi* were in fact used in homosexual contexts.[7] Actually, Dover seems to have overlooked the slogan we have already discussed in the *Laws* (636C) of Plato, in which Plato seems to assume that some form of female homosexuality exists.

Most of what little evidence exists, however, does come from the later period. We have discussed the slogans from Plutarch and Pseudo-Phocylides, which give no clues about any details. In

---

3. E.g., Dover, *Greek Homosexuality*, pp. 173–79; S. Pomeroy, *Goddesses, Whores, Wives, and Slaves: Women in Classical Antiquity* (New York: Schocken Books, 1975), pp. 53–56.
4. Dover, *Greek Homosexuality*, p. 172.
5. Plato, *Symposium* 191E, vol. III, LCL.
6. E.g., Pomeroy, *Goddesses, Whores, Wives, and Slaves*, plate no. 12.
7. E.g., Dover, *Greek Homosexuality*, plate R 223.

Plutarch's life of Lycurgus, the legendary legislator of Sparta, the mode of male relationships is the honorable pederastic one. This model was so esteemed, Plutarch writes, that it was imitated by the females, such that the young girls (*parthenai*) found lovers in beautiful and good women.[8] Thus at Sparta female homosexual relationships were of the same age differential as the male. As far as I know, this is the only suggestion that female homosexuality had such a differential. Even if the statement should be accurate historically, it would tell us nothing about female homosexuality in the period of Paul or Plutarch.

Clement of Alexandria, while reserving his scorn mostly for male pederasts, does include women by charging that they "play the man against nature, both being married and marrying women."[9] The words are sufficiently vague as to be, probably, intentionally unclear, but some form of female homosexuality is clearly implied, perhaps again with the use of *olisboi*.

More specific and yet still ambiguous is the paragraph in Pseudo-Lucian's *Erōtes*. Charicles, the defender of heterosexuality in the debate, makes his final argument: If it is proper for there to be pederasty, then it ought to be proper for women to love each other. The speaker clearly implies that the mode of such homosexuality is the use of the *olisboi*. "Let them strap to themselves cunningly contrived instruments of lechery, those mysterious monstrosities devoid of seed, and let woman lie with woman as does a man."[10]

Finally, there is the curious and tantalizingly ambiguous piece of Lucian in his *Dialogues of the Courtesans*.[11] Rumors have it that a courtesan, Leaena, is living with a woman, Megilla, who is in love with Leaena like a man (*hōsper andra*). Leaena then describes the seduction, in which Megilla and another woman lure her to bed with them after a drinking party. Megilla pulls off a wig, reveals herself as the "male" of the couple, and claims that the two women have been "married" for a long time. Megilla boasts to be

8. Plutarch, *Lycurgus* XVIII. 4.
9. Clement, *Paidagogos* III. iii. 21, 3, au. trans.
10. Pseudo-Lucian, *Erōtes* 28.
11. Lucian, *Dialogues of the Courtesans* 5.

a man, to have everything that a man does, or at least to have an appropriate substitute. Leaena gives in and the two presumably make love, but when Leaena is pressed for further details, she refuses and the dialogue ends abruptly.

Obviously Lucian is titillating the reader with the ambiguity of the language and the abrupt cutoff. If one had, however, to conclude what Lucian is implying about female homosexuality, some things would be clear. Female homosexuality is assumed to have the same division of roles as does pederasty. There is the active and the passive partner. Stimulation of the woman is achieved by a substitute for the male organ. That is, Lucian may assume that the model of female homosexuality follows at least in part that of pederasty. Whether, however, there is any age differential as in pederasty is impossible to say from this brief treatise.

What we should make of these few references is clouded further by the fact that everything is filtered through the eyes of the male authors. They at least acknowledge that female homosexuality exists, but they seem not to care much about it one way or the other. Given the isolation of many women from the male society of the day, it would not seem unlikely that close friendships among women would be made, even though Juvenal represents a woman claiming that such relationships did not happen, in contrast to the tawdry kinds of pederasty.[12]

If the *olisboi* figured as prominently in such encounters as the paintings and texts suggest, then the sexual dimension of female homosexuality was every bit as ambiguous as that of pederastic intercourse.[13] The prominence of the artificial phallus may just be, however, a fantasy of the male painters and authors, as if to say that even if women take to women, the only way they can be genuinely satisfied is through the male penis. About the most that can be said is that the male society of Paul's day *suspected* that female homosexuality existed and tended to interpret it along the lines of the kinds of pederastic and heterosexual relationships with which it was acquainted.

12. Juvenal, *Satire* II, lines 46–50.
13. But cf. Dover, *Greek Homosexuality*, plate R 207, where the stimulation is manual between two women.

ATTITUDES OF MALE AUTHORS
TOWARD FEMALE HOMOSEXUALITY

Even less can be said to this issue. Ovid portrays a woman in love with another as lamenting the unnaturalness of her passion.[14] But in general what few passages we have seem rather clear of judgment one way or the other. It may be important to note that the defender of heterosexuality in Pseudo-Lucian suggests that *if* men are going to engage in pederastic relationships, then it is to be expected that women will seek lovers among themselves. If one had to judge on the basis of our evidence I do not think Dover's suggestion that such homosexuality was a threat to the male ego could be substantiated. Perhaps from the claimed pedestal of male beauty the male society did not think female homosexuality important or interesting enough to worry about.

14. Ovid, *Metamorphoses* IX. 727–29.

Some Psychological Reflections

Greco-Roman homosexual culture, it is now obvious, had very specific societal contours quite different from our own twentieth-century homosexual models and patterns. Male and female homosexuals may claim today that they have only a single-sex preference, whether or not they engage in homosexual activities. This is for them a given, not a learned direction. They may feel they cannot change and they do not feel responsible for what is given. Some authors, as we have seen, distinguish between this given propensity to same-sex desire and the participation by persons of basically heterosexual orientation in homosexual activity.

Greco-Roman males, however, did not exhibit in general such a single-minded preference. From being a beloved as a boy by an adult male, they would in turn become adult lovers of boys. Many were by then married, or would marry. Some of the most infamous homosexuals were also thought to have had promiscuous relations with females as well.[1] Greco-Roman homosexuality was practiced by a large number of males because it was socially acceptable and, in some quarters, idealized as a normal course in the process of maturation. In sum, Greco-Roman male culture may be more a manifestation of bisexual expression than homosexual.

Sigmund Freud developed the thesis that there is a "constitutional bisexuality of each individual."[2] During the process of sexual organization, it is "normal" (i.e., it happens most often) that the boy will make his primary identification with the father and the girl with the mother and this, Freud thought, was influenced by "the relative strength of the masculine and feminine sexual dispositions."[3] The process of identification, however, is complex.

1. E.g., Timarchus; Aeschines, *Against Timarchus* 42.
2. Sigmund Freud, *The Ego and the Id* (London: The Hogarth Press, 1974), p. 21.
3. Ibid., p. 23.

"A boy has not merely an ambivalent attitude towards his father and an affectionate object-choice towards his mother, but at the same time he also behaves like a girl and displays an affectionate feminine attitude to his father and a corresponding jealousy and hostility towards his mother."[4] Thus for Freud, not only was bisexuality native to the infant, it continued to play a role through the stages of sexual organization—and doubtless throughout one's life, though normally in a completely repressed way.[5]

The expression or repression of one's bisexuality will then be finally determined by the larger culture into which the boy or girl moves. And it is clear that Greek culture *permitted the expression* rather than *demanded the repression* of male bisexuality.[6] In an insightful and provocative paper George Devereux has taken this basic insight and has explored Greek homosexual culture from a psychoanalytic perspective. The following paragraphs are entirely indebted to his argument.[7]

Devereux defines genuine perversion by three terms: stability, compulsion, and functional damper.[8] By stability he means that the condition is permanent; by compulsion, that the person has no control over his behavior and attitude; by damper, that one aim of perversion is "the reduction of the *intensity* of sexual experiences."[9] This last is desired because "in a perversion, the sexual drive is fused with and is in the service of nonsexual, aggressive drives."[10] Thus in his view perversion masks hostility and aggression. Presumably it is thus possible to detect a significant amount of repressed aggression in a case of perversion (although according to Freud all sexuality is fused with some aggression).

4. Ibid.
5. For a discussion and critique of Freud on these issues, cf. the paper by K. W. Freund, "Male Homosexuality: An Analysis of the Pattern," in *Understanding Homosexuality: Its Biological and Psychological Bases*, edited by J. A. Loraine (New York: American Elsevier Publishing Co., 1974), pp. 41–44.
6. I will not indulge in fantasy over the chicken and egg problem, whether culture created the homosexuality or vice versa. We are not concerned here with origins but with functions.
7. George Devereux, "Greek Pseudo-Homosexuality and the 'Greek Miracle,'" *Symbolae Osloenses* 42 (1968): 69–92.
8. Ibid., p. 72. Devereux uses the term "perversion" in a way entirely different from Bailey and McNeill cited above. In fact, by "perversion" he means what they mean by "inversion."
9. Ibid.
10. Ibid.

Appendix C

Devereux denies that Greek homosexuality exhibited these three traits. In his judgment the phenomenon is rather to be explained as a culturally prolonged "undifferentiated pubertal sexuality."[11] He writes: "The adolescent—and especially the pubescent—is not (*yet*) heterosexual *or* homosexual; he is simply sexual."[12] What happened in Greek culture is that the stage of the "simply sexual adolescent"—a stage which is usually temporary and short-lived—was permitted to last long after it was transcended in most cultures. With the approbation of youth, and especially the beautiful youth, which we have already seen to be so strong in this culture, it is not surprising that males wished to hold onto that stage as long as possible. This was not only true for the youth; it is also manifested in the adult lover, who by his relationship with his youthful beloved maintained contact with that stage of undifferentiated sexuality.

In Devereux's judgment this does not explain entirely the adult-youth relationship, since youths might have related to each other as well as adults with adults. He thinks the answer here lies in the presumed inadequacy of the natural father to be a genuine father. The adult lover thus becomes a substitute for the father— Devereux calls it "displaced fathering."[13] "In most societies, the father is responsible for the misbehavior of his son; in Sparta, characteristically, it was the *erastēs* [the adult lover] who was responsible for the *erōmenos'* [the youth's] misconduct. Displaced fathering can hardly go to greater extremes."[14]

Devereux does not believe that the Greek male was permanently homosexual. The male went through certain stages— beloved, lover, married man. This process of moving eventually to heterosexuality Devereux calls "sliding" and he points to a number of examples of how this sliding was made easier for the emerging heterosexual male.[15] For example, on the assumption that pederastic intercourse was normally anal, he cites the late evidence of Athenaeus that in classical Sparta boys had intercourse with young girls anally before it was time for them to marry.[16] If

11. Ibid., p. 73.
12. Ibid., p. 75.
13. Ibid., p. 78,
14. Ibid., p. 79.
15. Ibid., pp. 82f.
16. Ibid., pp. 83f.

147

this source is to be trusted, it would indicate that male youths, accustomed to being entered in this fashion themselves, would begin to explore heterosexual relations in the manner with which they were familiar.

According to another source to which Devereux refers, the Spartan bride had her head shaven and was dressed in male clothes. The original sexual encounters with the bride then occurred at night on visits of the youth to the bride's home, in complete darkness, so that at the beginning the two did not actually see each other.[17] This was, perhaps, another dimension of the Spartan technique of sliding.

Devereux does not seem to have noticed what has been mentioned above, that the image of youthful beauty changed over the centuries, from heavily "masculine" to sensuously "feminine." That might be interpreted also as a subtle process of sliding. The adult lover now seeks a youth to love who is closer in form to the female he will later encounter.

From an entirely different direction comes, perhaps, some support for the claim that Greek homosexuality was essentially bisexual. In an analysis of male homosexuality, K. W. Freund has studied bodily preferences among several groups of males. He concludes that "in males who erotically prefer physically mature partners there is virtually no bisexuality, in terms of responses to body shape. . . . Contrary to that, such a conspicuously high degree of bisexuality in terms of responses to body shape *did appear in some paedophilic or paedo-ephebophilic males*."[18] That is, it is precisely those adult males who prefer younger males and boys who are most likely to be bisexual.[19]

A number of questions should be raised about Devereux's use of evidence and the conclusions he draws from it.

1. It is not certain, in my judgment, that a married male ceased to have pederastic relationships. Nor do I find evidence that all adult lovers married. That some did does not prove the point. There is often sharp hostility expressed toward women on the

17. Ibid., p. 84. The source is Plutarch, *Lycurgus* XV. 3.
18. Freund, "Male Homosexuality," p. 44, italics mine. He defines his terms: "Paedophilia is the erotic preference for children, ephebophilia that for male . . . pubescents," p. 44.
19. Freund admits that at this stage of research his conclusions are suggestive but not definitive.

part of the adult male lovers. Whether such hostility would be overcome or whether it might effectively inhibit the sliding and turn males into permanent bachelors ever in search of the lovely male youth is an open question.

2. Devereux's claim that Greek fathers were not good ones is based on slight evidence. It *may* have been true and thus may have been one dynamic in structuring that particular configuration of pederasty. But it is not necessary for the argument. The idealization of youth (as he notes) is sufficient cause for the adult's constant attention to youths, while the youths or boys would accept the patterns (*a*) because it was expected of them and (*b*) they received benefits from adults other youths could not offer them, both monetary and educational.

3. The assumption that anal intercourse was normal in pederastic relations that included sexual involvement is probably correct, but Dover's recent investigation raises certain doubts. The vase paintings, upon which Dover's argument depends, do in fact show the pederastic embrace as intercrural, only in rare instances as anal. It must be remembered, however, that these vase paintings are quite early and in no way give evidence for the majority of the centuries we are considering.

4. Dover's arguments affect another conclusion of Devereux. Dover thinks that anal intercourse in the society was seen as an aggressive and at times humiliating act.[20] To the extent that pederastic sexual encounters were anal, a certain amount of aggression might be present, contrary to Devereux's admittedly qualified judgment.[21]

But these questions affect only details; they do not call into question the basic psychoanalytic insights of Devereux or his conclusion that Greek homosexuality is not "perversion" (or inversion) but a prolongation of sexually undifferentiated adolescence. The conclusion is thus probably justified: Greek male culture was basically bisexual in character.

---

20. Dover, *Greek Homosexuality*, p. 105.
21. "On the whole, there is no evidence that the Greek homosexual . . . contained *considerable* amounts of aggressivity and hostility fused with sexuality," Devereux, "Greek Pseudo-Homosexuality," p. 73, italics his.

Index of Passages

BIBLE

Index

Index

Index of Authors
and Subjects

D'Youville College Library
320 Porter Avenue
Buffalo, New York 14201